I0568828

OPERATION TRICKERY

Deception During WWII

RECOMMENDED

JAMES HOWELL

Copyright @2021 by James Howell

All rights reserved. No part of this book may be reproduced in any form or by any electronic or mechanical means, including information storage and retrieval systems, without permission in writing from the publisher, except by reviewers, who may quote brief passages in a review.

This publication contains the opinions and ideas of its author. It is intended to provide helpful and informative material on the subjects addressed in the publication. The author and publisher specifically disclaim all responsibility for any liability, loss or risk, personal or otherwise, which is incurred as a consequence, directly or indirectly, of the use and application of any of the contents of this book.

WORKBOOK PRESS LLC
187 E Warm Springs Rd,
Suite B285, Las Vegas, NV 89119, USA

Website: https://workbookpress.com/
Hotline: 1-888-818-4856
Email: admin@workbookpress.com

Ordering Information:
Quantity sales. Special discounts are available on quantity purchases by corporations, associations, and others.
For details, contact the publisher at the address above.

Library of Congress Control Number:
ISBN-13:   978-1-956017-93-9 (Paperback Version)
              978-1-956017-94-6 (Digital Version)

REV. DATE: 11/04/2021

OPERATION TRICKERY

TRICKERY

DECEPTION DURING WWII

JAMES HOWELL

COPYRIGHT © 2019 BY JAMES HOWELL.

LIBRARY OF CONGRESS CONTROL NUMBER:		2019916688
ISBN:	HARDCOVER	978-1-7960-6648-7
	SOFTCOVER	978-1-7960-6647-0
	EBOOK	978-1-7960-6646-3

All rights reserved. No part of this book may be reproduced or transmitted in any form or by any means, electronic or mechanical, including photocopying, recording, or by any information storage and retrieval system, without permission in writing from the copyright owner.

This is a work of fiction. Names, characters, places and incidents either are the product of the author's imagination or are used fictitiously, and any resemblance to any actual persons, living or dead, events, or locales is entirely coincidental.

Any people depicted in stock imagery provided by Getty Images are models, and such images are being used for illustrative purposes only.
Certain stock imagery © Getty Images.

Rev. date: 10/17/2019

Xlibris
1-888-795-4274
www.Xlibris.com

795657

CONTENTS

Foreword

Operation Trickery is not part of James Howell's first three books about the race to build the first atomic bomb but does incorporate many of the same characters.

The three main characters are Colonel Powers, Blake Runnels and Nate Simmons. Colonel Powers is the leader of a small group of journalists brought together to observe, record and report all observations in the battlefield to aid the Allies drive the Axis forces out of North Africa, Malta, Sicily and eventually Italy.

Operation Trickery did not win any battles but did help demoralize Axis forces and created enough chaos to help win the battle to drive Axis forces out of North Africa.

Chapter 1

90 MILES FROM NOWHERE

Blake Runnels and Nate Simmons were sleeping off a beer drunk when the telephone began to ring. The ringing was loud enough to shake the rafters in the ceiling of the small cabin. It was three o'clock in the morning of April 10, 1941. The fishermen were in their cabin near the Gila Wilderness in Southwestern New Mexico, 90 miles from nowhere.

Blake uncovered his head just long enough to shout at Nate, "It's for you!" He didn't know who was calling, but he did know he did not want to crawl out of his warm bedroll, cross the 10 feet of cold wooden floor just to answer the annoying telephone. It was too cold, too early, too dark, and too everything to answer the damn ringing nuisance.

Early April in the Cibola National Forest was beautiful but cold. Snow falls above 7,000 feet this time of year, but the mountain streams were already full of hungry trout. The cold clear water was the best breeding ground for young trout, and they were biting at wintered bugs as they began to appear.

Nate ripped the cover off his bedroll and bound across the cold cabin floor to grab the black telephone receiver. In the dark and cold, Nate's reaction was automatic. It had been eleven years since he left the navy. He was a navy special services leader, and he learned quickly to react without thinking or to consider the consequences. In his haste to respond quickly, he became freezing cold. It didn't take long for him to realize he had been "had" by his old friend Blake hiding under the warm covers. He and Blake were friends for more years than he could remember. The two friends were journalists for the *Mountain Mail*, a monthly newsletter that served the mountainous region around Socorro and Magdalena, New Mexico. The paper began publishing the *Mail* in 1893 and had closed unexpectedly recently, leaving the pair unemployed. It was rumored that a new owner was to reopen the paper soon.

Although Nate was angry and cold, he decided to answer the still-ringing telephone. "Who is this?" he barked into the cold receiver.

"Good morning, Nate. This is Colonel Powers." It was a pleasant response to Nate's rude question. "How are you? What are you doing in the wilderness?"

"Oh sorry, sir, I have a headache, and it's cold, and we are fishing."

"What do you have planned for the day?" Colonel Powers asked.

"Blake and I are trout fishing. It's cold, dark, and I am going back to bed for another week to get rid of this beer hangover."

Colonel Powers pleaded. "I need you both again for an Alsos mission to travel to the beautiful Mediterranean . . ." There was a short pause before he continued. "Forget the trout. We have bigger fish to fry. I need you and Blake to meet me in Houston on the twelfth."

"What is so important that we should drop our fishing trip and meet you in Houston?" Nate responded while rubbing his throbbing temples.

"I'm sorry, old friend," Colonel Powers said in desperation. "This is not an order from the army, it's from your old commander. A civilian organization is needing our help in the North Africa campaign. They have a couple of little jobs and secret missions that you should enjoy. Especially the scenery and food . . ." Another pause followed with no response from Nate. "You will enjoy the surroundings, and it shouldn't be dangerous. I just need your eyes and ears to record the missions."

"Did you say it shouldn't be dangerous?" Nate asked. "That is what you said about our last little job that almost got us killed several times . . ." After another pause, Nate continued. "Anyway, you haven't said the magic word yet."

Colonel Powers smiled into the receiver and said the magic word. "All right, PLEASE, and I owe you a beer and hamburger."

"Tell me more about this little job. I'll have to discuss it with Blake before we agree to meet with you."

"It's classified. I can't tell you more about the mission until I meet with you in Houston. I can tell you the mission is critical to driving the Axis powers out of North Africa and to invade Mainland Europe . . ." Powers paused before pleading with Nate. "I really need your help, and I need an answer now."

"I can't speak for Blake, but I will be there," Nate responded. "I bet Blake will be there too since he and Vivian are fighting again. That's why we're fishing."

Nate ended his conversation with Powers and slipped back into his bedroll. He hadn't been in bed thirty seconds before Blake uncovered his head to ask who was calling. Nate blurted out the name of Powers and continued to try to go back to sleep.

"What did he want?" Blake asked.

"I'll tell you in the morning. Go back to sleep." Nate answered before falling to sleep.

The sun rises early at 7,000 feet in the Cibola National Forest. The Beaverhead Ranger station next to Blake's cabin is just below the tree line, and the aspen were still dormant. The snow is beginning to melt, but wouldn't keep the two fishermen from fishing. They had plenty of beer antifreeze.

Blake's aunt Anabel built the cabin in 1930 as part of her two-section homestead that straddled the Continental Divide in the Pelona Mountains. She deserted the cabin and homestead after two cold winters at 9,200 feet elevation and moved back to Oklahoma and more comfortable temperatures. The cabin remained deserted for several years until she donated it to the Beaverhead Ranger Station for a fire lookout. The rangers built a 110-foot steel tower next to the cabin to watch for forest fires in the Cibola National Forest and Gila Wilderness. From the top of the tower, a person could see traffic on US Highway 60, some 55 miles north.

A telephone in the area is rare. The only use of the instrument is to report forest fires to officials in Socorro and Las Cruces or to make emergency calls to ranger station personnel. Blake convinced the Beaverhead Ranger Station supervisor to allow the two anglers access to the cabin during the off season in exchange for watching for forest fires while they fish. The cabin isn't much, but it did shield the two men from the wind and cold nights. It is vacant during the winter and reopened in June for the summer, when most fires occurred caused by lightning strikes. Arson is virtually unheard of in these mountains.

To occupy their time, they fished for trout. They spent half their time fishing and the other half drinking beer and watching for forest fires from the tower. Wheeled vehicles are not permitted in the Gila Wilderness. In the nearby Cibola National Forest, there are no camping facilities, which limited the vacationing traffic. It is quiet and isolated—just the way they liked it.

It is 90 miles to a doctor or hospital in Magdalena.

Blake recalled the book his aunt had written in 1932 titled *90 Miles from Nowhere*. The title was fitting for the location, isolated and bordering the Gila Wilderness where the Gila Indian Cliff Dwellings were abandoned hundreds of years earlier.

Blake couldn't sleep after hearing that Colonel Powers had called. He could not imagine how the colonel found them in the forest. He had not told anyone, except his wife Vivian, that he and Nate were going fishing. Nate also confirmed that he had not told anyone of their trip. He finally deduced that Powers had called his home in Socorro where Vivian gave him the number to the ranger station. He was missing his wife even though they had fought over something he couldn't remember. It was always something insignificant. All the deep thinking finally resulted in short spells of fitful sleep.

The next morning Blake was up early to make some coffee and cook some eggs and fresh trout. Nate could not resist the aroma of trout on the fire and fresh coffee. He finally climbed out of bed and approached Blake at the fireplace. "Smells great—trout, coffee, eggs, and biscuits. If you were prettier, I would marry you."

"Don't get your hopes up, I have better taste than a navy swab." Blake responded while pouring himself a second cup of coffee and one for Nate.

"What did Powers want last night?" Blake asked. "Did he want us to do something for him that would get us killed?"

"You are very perceptive this morning," Nate answered. "He needs us to meet him in Houston on the twelfth for a little trip to the Mediterranean."

"Are you kidding? He must be out of his mind if he thinks I will drop everything and join him on one of his crazy missions. I've had enough war games. Let someone else do his dirty work."

"I knew you felt that way," Nate responded. "I have already planned our trip to Houston and told Powers that you would be there, especially since you and Vivian are fighting again." Nate explained as he moved away from Blake, yielding the heavy frying pan.

"If I didn't have the last piece of trout in this pan, I would find a place to put it where you would never smile again," Blake responded. "The only reason I would agree to meet with Powers is to avoid more fighting with Vivian," Blake continued. "You knew that before you committed me anyway, didn't you?"

Chapter 2

SAN FRANCISCO: IT STARTED HERE

Colonel Powers made two calls in San Francisco: the first to Dino Tanaka and second to John Anello. Both men worked with the Alsos mission in the past and were needed again.

Currently, John was working with the Federal Bureau of Investigation in the Northern California area, while Dino lives and works in Sacramento as a journalist. Both men served with the mission in Europe, where they were assigned to work with the Italian resistance and the Chinese Army in Korea as journalists and, occasionally, as saboteurs and kidnappers—not exactly the work of either a journalist or civil servant.

Convincing John and Dino to rejoin the Alsos mission would not be easy. It was dangerous working with the Italian underground and especially the Chinese Army. Colonel Powers knew he could not order either of the men to join him in the mission, but he also knew they were desperately needed. In addition, he knew both men made many close friends in Italy and China and even a long-distance love affair with a beautiful Italian underground leader. Both men would probably decline an offer to rejoining the mission based on friendship alone. He needed a little leverage.

Colonel Powers contacted both John's and Dino's supervisors in Washington and Sacramento before contacting the two men to explain their absences and the importance of their assignments. Both supervisors agreed to allow them to take extended vacations but could not order them to accept the invitation. Both supervisors were told nothing of their assignments, except that they were top secret and very important to the advancement of the Allied forces in the war.

It was time to contact John and Dino.

"Don't answer the phone."

John was at home when the telephone rang. His lovely roommate made him answer anyway. "Hello, this is John Anello. Who may I say is calling?"

Surprised at the formality of John's telephone manner, Colonel Powers answered.

"Hi, John, this is Colonel Powers. How are you? What have you been doing?"

"Good morning, Colonel. It is good to hear from you. Are you enjoying your new Washington job?" The response came effortlessly, like talking to an old friend, but John felt uncomfortable and did not know why. He was still in bed with a headache from last night's party. "What can I do for you, Colonel?"

"I'm glad you asked, I have a favor to ask," Powers responded. "Can you meet me at Duce's Diner in an hour?"

"Sure, I can, if you agree to buy breakfast and if you promise to keep me out of the war, and what is so important that we can't discuss it over the telephone?"

"It's classified, John."

John agreed to meet at the café in an hour. He was reluctant at first but knew he could not refuse Colonel Powers' request. After hearing of the mission. It was an offer John had wanted since his last Alsos mission assignment—another mission into enemy territory with the likelihood of active combat and shelling, foreigners and friendly people alike firing various deadly weapons at you, the horrible living conditions and often no food or canned food. Powers could not promise to keep him safe and out of the war, but he did promise him exotic travel, better food, and even some old friends to keep him company.

John reluctantly accepted Powers' proposal because he felt compelled to help in the war effort. He was comfortable working with the FBI in California and did not relish the extended travel and possible enemy fire, but he accepted when Powers described the personnel involved, especially his friend Dino.

"I knew I shouldn't have answered the phone," John responded.

"I'm to contact Dino next, any suggestions?" Colonel Powers asked.

"Yes, be nice and mention Nora and the Italian underground. He may resist, but he can't wait to see her again." John replied.

"Come with me," Colonel Powers suggested. "He will be glad to see you again. He may not respond favorably to me."

John declined to accompany Powers to meet Dino. "You are on your own, he is a friend of mine and I want it to stay that way. Besides he loves you for kidnapping him for your first little mission," John continued. "You know he can't refuse since you were responsible for saving him and his family from that nasty camp holding everyone with a Japanese sounding name. Even those citizens that had been born here."

John was right. Just the mention of Nora and the Italian underground convinced Dino to join the mission. Colonel Powers' proposition was too much for Dino to resist, and Dino officially accepted the invitation to join the mission without hesitation. Dino's supervisor had also helped convince him that the mission to help end the war was in his best interest.

The three men were to meet again in London with a contingent of other members of the mission thus far unnamed for security reasons.

Colonel Powers had to promise to have John and Dino work with the Italian resistance following a short assignment in the Egyptian desert. "Why the Egyptian desert?" John asked. "What could possibly be of interest in the desert?"

"We need your eyes and ears to confirm or deny enemy information."

San Francisco Airport Meeting

"What have we gotten ourselves into?" John asked as he embraced his old friend Dino at the airport.

"I'm not sure, but it's good to see you again. It will be good to see and work with Enzo and Nora again too . . ." After a pause, Dino continued. "Colonel Powers has promised to keep us safe, but I can't imagine anywhere that is safe in North Africa and Italy."

"I know Nate and Blake will be working with us again. I hope Sergeants Davis and Martinez will join us too." John added.

"Let's get some coffee and a sandwich, it is a long flight to New York," Dino said. "But not as long as the second leg to London and then to our assignment."

"I guess we will be told where we will be assigned at the briefing in London and meet the other members of the team," John added. "Exciting, but I have too many questions to be comfortable enough to have fun."

"Really good to see you again. Hopefully, we will be able to work with the Italian underground again."

"Good to see you too," Dino said while the two men moved to the departing flight to New York. "Any idea what we will be doing in the Mediterranean? Powers wasn't clear about where we were going or what we would be doing. It just sounded dangerous and secretive, a typical Powers mission."

"I guess we will find out at our briefing in London," John said while the two men took their seats for the long flight to New York. "Six hours to New York, change planes, and another ten hours, we should be in London. Sounds more like Powers all the time."

"It will give you a chance to read, and I can take a little nap," Dino said. "Have you heard from any of your old friends from the Italian underground or Nora?" Dino inquired.

"I was wondering when you would mention Nora," John said. "You two got pretty thick just before we left Italy. Hopefully, we will work with the same group as we did in Genoa, including Nora and her brother."

"I will never forget the transformation Nora went through—one day in a beautiful yellow sun dress discussing health care and the next evening in baggy fatigues as the leader of the Italian resistance in Northern Italy—quite a change." Dino said.

Chapter 3

Alsos Headquarters Briefing

Colonel Powers met the two men from San Francisco at the luggage claim area. "You guys look terrible!" Powers exclaimed. "You look like you have slept in those clothes for two days."

"Funny you should say that, that's exactly what we did," John explained. "Seems more like a week flying time and crossing the International Date Line."

Colonel Powers pumped the hands of both men from San Francisco and promised to give them time to rest, have a good meal before their scheduled briefing. "Really good to see you guys again."

"Where is your uniform?" Dino asked. "You look more like a civilian than an army colonel."

"Good guess, you will be dressed this way too," Powers said. "Civilian clothes everywhere, except for the few times working with the British. Save your questions until the briefing at 0630 hours tomorrow. And don't be late."

"Is it always wet and dark here?" John asked. "The only times I have been here it is wet, dark, and miserable."

"That's probably because it is 0330 hours here," Powers explained. "Don't worry, you won't be here long enough to get used to the weather. Your flight will leave London at 1830 hours tomorrow.

"I guess my plan to see London will have to wait. Kind of a tight schedule." John exclaimed.

Two days later, the two men from San Francisco were to arrive in Alexandria and bound for something called the Depression in the desert southwest of the airport.

"That was the shortest and most intense briefing I have ever witnessed," John said as they walked toward baggage-claim to meet their OSS contact.

Chapter 4

WHO ELSE WILL BE JOINING US?

"I was wondering why the heck my boss told me to take some time off," Dino said. "Did your supervisor tell you to take a vacation too?"

Neither John nor Dino were particularly busy at present, and the war was draining men and machinery from all areas of the country for the war, but also, the FBI was busy doing stuff not related to John's responsibilities. And Dino had been slowly working himself out of a job with fewer weddings or obituaries to report. "Powers must have contacted our bosses, what do you think?" John asked even though he knew the answer.

As the colonel described their missions, the everyday activity should not involve direct battle contact but simply reporting results of enemy activity and coordinate Allied efforts—sounded simple enough. Unfortunately, Colonel Powers failed to mention the necessary contact with OSS agents in Alexandria and Oran and the necessary message drops to OSS and British agents behind enemy lines. He decided to keep the details of their assignments simple and uncomplicated, mainly to keep them from refusing the assignments, and they probably wouldn't understand the complexities of the operations anyway. "Keep it simple, stupid."

Powers Calls to Sgts. Martinez and Davis

Colonel Powers had two other calls to make: the first to El Paso, Texas, and Sergeant Martinez and the second to Sergeant Davis in Chicago, Illinois. Neither man would be glad to hear from the colonel. They had been discharged from active duty before the outbreak of war in Europe, but wartime changed that. Many noncommissioned officers released from the army before 1941 were told to return to active duty. Martinez and Davis were to report to the Headquarters in London for their assignments on April 14th at 0630. Colonel Powers' calls to both men were unwelcomed and yet not a complete surprise.

The addition of the two military personnel completed the Alsos mission in North Africa.

Chapter 5

WHERE'S NATE

"Where's Nate?" Colonel Powers asked Blake while gathering his luggage at the Houston airport. "We don't have any time to lose. Is he lost again?"

"Another beer headache and trip to the head," Blake answered. "He should be here any minute now, and it's good to see you again."

"Sorry, I'm a little rattled because of our tight schedule. It's good to see you too," Colonel Powers finally slowed down long enough to apologize to his old friend. "I wasn't sure if Vivian would let you leave Socorro to join our party," Powers said. "So I guess you and Vivian are still fighting, or you caught your limit of trout. You should love the food and people where you're going."

"Why are you out of uniform?" Blake asked the colonel dressed in blue jeans, sweater, and baseball cap. "I thought you were back in the army stationed in Washington."

"I am still in the army and stationed in Washington but working with a civilian group," Powers answered. "We will all be working in various areas, and modes of dress depending on your location, and you won't be working in American uniforms," Powers continued as Nate approached the two men gathering luggage. "Bad water again?" Powers asked.

"Yeah," Nate answered. "I should know better by now that water is not good for me. Beer keeps me regular and better hydrated and doesn't rust my pipes like water does." Nate continued while shaking Powers' hand and removing his dark glasses to expose red eyes and many new wrinkles.

"What is so important that you drag us down here for a meeting?" Blake asked as the three men moved to an army green sedan waiting at the curb at the main entrance to the Houston airport.

"I'll explain on our way to Corpus Christi Naval Air Station," Powers said. "I'm sure you guys remember your last flight out of the naval air station, we're heading back to RAF Mendenhall, just like last time. Our new Headquarters is next door to British Intelligence MI6 in Downtown London."

Powers explained the importance and classified nature of their new missions to the surprise of both Nate and Blake.

"When do we start?" Nate asked. "Will Sergeants Martinez and Davis be joining our little party, and what about John and Dino?"

Powers explained that their assignments would be made during the briefing at Alsos Headquarters the next day.

"Didn't you say that we would not be in any danger?" Blake asked. "From what I hear, it sounds like we could be shot anytime by multiple countries. The Germans and Italians will not look kindly to our intrusion onto their battle grounds. Even the Vichy French troops will not be friendly."

"You will be in native dress surrounded by millions of miles of desert sand and probably have to search for a battle to record." Powers continued. "Your job will be to record the battles that you see or hear about, remain in native clothing, and avoid any direct contact with the enemy."

"Doesn't sound safe to me either," Nate echoed Blake's sentiments. "I bet you want us to work with both the Italian and French undergrounds. We could be shot. There is no way you can guarantee our safety."

"You're starting to sound like sissies," Powers said. "What happened to the guys that were at ground zero when the first atomic bomb test was detonated and the guys who captured Dr. Heisenberg in Hechingen just before the Russians invaded the area?" Powers paused for effect then continued. "Not up to a little challenge while on vacation in the beautiful Mediterranean? It should be fun. The stuff you can tell your grandkids . . . There are two dangers you must be aware of." Powers said. "The first is the hot regional foods and the belly dancers. At least the Russians won't be pushing you around."

Powers turned to the back seat to face Nate and Blake heavy snoring. "Don't seem overly concerned now," Colonel Powers said to himself. The two friends finally succumbed to sleep at the rhythm of the tires and the monotony of Powers' warnings.

Five hours later, the sedan entered the main gate to the Corpus Christi Naval Air Station. "Rise and shine, boys," Powers said to the two sleeping buddies. His first reaction was to use the typical saying about sleeping beauties, but it really did not apply to these two old friends. They were still ugly as sin. "Our flight to RAF Mendenhall will leave in an hour. Grab a sandwich and some coffee, it will be about twelve hours for your next chance to eat anything."

The Lockheed A-29 Hudson lifted off the Texas tarmac and landed the next day at RAF Mendenhall just south of Cambridge. Hungry and exhausted, the three men left for Downtown London and the Alsos Headquarters building.

"The mess hall is on the second floor down the hall from your rooms," Powers said. "The briefing will begin at 0630 hours. Be there at 0615 hours. Martinez and Davis will join us later for their assignments. Unfortunately, John and Dino will join the team later."

Blake and Nate devoured more mediocre food and drink as if the best French chef had prepared it. Still exhausted and suffering from travel and time fatigue, the two men made their way to the briefing at the appointed time of 0615 hours. "I hope this briefing won't last long; I'm fading fast." Nate said while following Blake to the briefing room.

Sergeants Martinez and Davis were waiting at the door to the briefing room as Nate and Blake approached. "Well, look who the cat dragged in!" Martinez exclaimed as the four old friends met.

"Yeah, good to see you old buzzards too," Nate said while shaking the hands of the two old friends from previous missions. "Easy, don't shake too hard or speak too loudly, my head hurts. Where's the colonel? He told us to be here early for the briefing."

"Do you know what we are doing here?" Sergeant Davis asked. "Our orders just told us to report to this room in this building in London today at 0800 hours. You said something about a colonel, could that be Colonel Powers?"

"I know, for sure, that Colonel Powers is involved," Blake explained. "The briefing will clarify what we be doing here, and it will probably involve travel to North Africa."

As the four old friends discussed their possible new assignments, the colonel approached the four men. "Good morning, gentlemen, right on time. Are you ready to see where you will be going and what your new jobs will be?" Colonel Powers continued. "Martinez and Davis will join us later. You two get some breakfast, and we can meet at 0800 hours as your orders say?" Colonel Powers directed as the two sergeants moved away toward the mess hall. "Grab a cup of coffee, this will take some time, and your flights will leave London late this afternoon," Colonel Powers said. "Before I begin, I must remind you that anything said here stays here. No communication home or telephone calls to girlfriends. Your location and duties are classified for your protection as well as many others. The only communications will be by radio between the two teams and this headquarters. Do not discuss your jobs or locations with anyone, except this headquarters. Loose lips sink ships is a truism here, and any infraction could cost your lives."

"Sir, you mentioned two teams. Who's on the team?" Blake asked.

"You, Nate, and Sergeant Martinez are team 1, while John, Dino, and Sergeant Davis are team 2." Powers said. "You will be assigned to various British and American forces but work independently. There will be times when you will work with an OSS or British MI6 agent for logistical assistance. Otherwise, you will work on your own."

"Sir, I thought the spooks at OSS just worked in intelligence-gathering like MI6. Why should we work with them?" Nate asked.

"Good question, Nate." Powers answered. "The areas you are

going will be foreign to you. The OSS will help you with local customs, clothing, food, and movement throughout the areas. You could face German, Italian, and Vichy French troops and the various countries' militias in your travels and performance of your duties. It is dangerous to work in these areas without OSS support. Let's take a quick break while I finish your assignments. I'll be back in fifteen minutes." Powers said as he left the briefing.

At 0800 Sergeants Martinez and Davis joined the briefing. "Take your seats and let's begin." Powers said while adding more papers to the various piles placed in front of each of the team members.

"Most of the information in front of you will apply to your assignments by team and geographical location. The large envelope contains several passports, cash for each country, radio contact information, maps, and the names of OSS and MI6 agents assigned to each team." Powers added.

"It will be necessary for you to memorize the information inside the file folder, and we will destroy it before you leave today. Each team will have two radios in case one fails. The contents of the large envelope will be concealed in your clothing. Your clothing can be carried in an old leather bag assigned to each team member," Powers continued. "Blake will direct team 1, while John will direct team 2 . . ." Powers paused before taking questions.

"I have one, sir," Sergeant Martinez responded. "How will we be moving about in our assigned areas?"

"Good question," Powers said. "We don't know yet. Each team will arrive at their assigned areas at different times and by different modes of transportation. That is where OSS and MI6 agents come into play. They will provide vehicles and clothing as needed. Did I forget to mention that each of you will be assigned a model 1911 Remington .45-caliber automatic pistol?" Powers continued after letting the groans and giggles die down. "The OSS will help with any other weapons you might need."

"Okay, start your memorizing," Powers added. "Sandwiches and drinks are coming here for lunch and the information destroyed by 1600 hours. When you are dismissed, pack your bags and change into the clothing provided for your trip to your assigned areas. Sergeant Douglas will direct you to your departure areas at 1900 hours," Powers said. "Good luck and be careful not to ruin any of that government-issued equipment and clothing."

"Do I have to wear this stupid towel on my head? Nate asked.

"If you don't your Bedouin neighbors will be suspicious." Colonel Powers added with a grin.

Chapter 6

OFF THE COAST OF LIBYA

The British submarine *Unshaken* approached the Libyan coastal village of Bin Jawwad in the early morning hours of April 16, 1941. It was a cool 50-something degrees, no moon, and only a slight southerly breeze, surprisingly cool after the afternoon high of 110 degrees. It was perfect for the two men posing as OSS agents as they boarded a small raft in the water off the coast. The two men were Blake Runnels and Nate Simons of past Alsos mission operations in Europe and the Pacific theater. Their mission was to watch and report the results of Allied and Axis subversive missions during the North African campaign. The two men were assigned to the British Army, wore British uniforms, but were working independently and reported directly to the London Alsos Headquarters and Colonel Powers.

Communication between the Allied forces was confusing. Many native languages were in use in the 2,000-mile-long battlefront from Egypt to Morocco. Communications worsened when working with the French and Italian undergrounds and their antiquated communications. Luckily for the Allies, there were English-, Italian-, and French-speaking interpreters readily available everywhere. Unfortunately for the Allies, the German High Command used the same languages to interfere with Allied communications. In addition, the Germans had developed a technique to find and destroy Allied radios by "triangulation." By monitoring radios from three points, the Germans could accurately locate Allied radios and made radio communications dangerous. Once detected, the German forces responded quickly to capture and destroy the radios and operators.

Nate was first to enter the small rubber boat from the deck of the submarine. "Hurry, searchlights have begun scanning the skies."

Blake couldn't move any faster, slowed by the monstrous pile of supplies on the deck to be loaded into the boat. "You could lend a hand here instead of staring at the sky . . . What's the rush? We're early," Blake responded. "Martinez probably will be late anyway." he added as he continued loading the supplies.

"I'll bet a six-pack he isn't waiting for us, and he will probably lose the way to the lave fields."

"Why are we going to that lava pile anyway?" Blake asked.

"The Al Haruj al Aswad lava field is a perfect position for our campsite," Nate responded. "It is isolated, quiet, and still close to tank traffic through the village of Al Fugaha. Even the Germans would not suspect anyone would operate a radio from the fields usually occupied only by Bedouins." Tired of Blake's questions, Nate said. "Stop complaining and get in the boat."

As the two men entered the water, more lights could be seen pointing their lighted fingers into the air, searching for enemy planes. The Allies had provided a diversion, hoping to attract the lights into the air away from the submarine in the waters off the coast. The submarine quickly disappeared beneath the water and safely headed into the deeper waters of the Mediterranean. Nate and Blake were alone in the still waters in their heavily-equipped craft some 500 yards off the beach.

"Where the heck is Martinez?" Nate asked in desperation.

Chapter 7

ITALIAN MORTAR FIRE

"Incoming!" a British soldier shouted a split second before the Italian mortar shell scored a direct hit on the wood and dirt bunker where John worked.

Several moments later, John stirred under a blanket of dust when the shelling stopped. His head hurt, and his ears rang loud enough to wake him from the worst of nightmares. As he tried to open his eyes, the dust in the air clouded his vision. Everything moved slowly as if mired in some unseen glue or heavy fog. As his vision cleared, he stared at the profile of his head and shoulders outlined on his desk in the dust.

Dino ran into the dusty bunker to find John seated at the small writing desk staring at his hat. "Are you hurt?"

John was seated at the desk and covered his head with his hands as the explosion shook the bunker. His baseball cap had fallen from his head and lay on its side covered in dust. He marveled that it was backward with the bill pointed in the wrong direction. "That's weird," he said, and he laughed.

Dino repeated his question. "Are you hurt?"

John heard the distant voice of someone calling his name but didn't recognize it through the mental fog and ringing in his ears.

"What?" he asked, coughing and sneezing through the dust. He turned to find Dino staring at him in disbelief.

"You look like a ghost," Dino said while waving his hands in front of his own face to chase the dust from his vision.

"You like toast?" John responded through his confusion.

"No, you look like a ghost," Dino repeated, louder this time.

"I don't understand. Do I want some toast?"

"No, you look like—never mind," Dino said in frustration, trying to understand the confusion and hearing loss suffered by John.

John shook his head to remove the dust and fog from his slowly returning vision while pointing to his ear where the ringing persisted. "I can't hear you," As he tried to stand, he fell back into his chair.

Dino helped John to the cot in the corner of the bunker. "Stay here, I'll find help!" Dino shouted as he left the damaged bunker in search of a medic.

There were injured British soldiers in line, standing, sitting, and lying on the ground, waiting for the few medics available and very busy. John's injuries were described to the medic busy placing a tourniquet on a soldier's leg missing a foot. "Let me see if I have this right—your friend is confused and lost his hearing, and you want me to stop trying to save this guy's leg to fix your friend's hearing?"

Dino recognized the serious nature of the work of the medic and decided to attend to John's wounds himself. Simple hearing loss was not an emergency compared to the soldiers' injuries.

*   *   *

John remained seated on the cot, trying to shake the dust from his hair and clothing as Dino returned to the bunker. The dust in the bunker had settled on Dino's back and on one side of his face. The front of his fatigues and the other half of his face were clean. Dino looked terrible and silly at the same time.

"You look like half a ghost," Dino said. "Can you hear me now?"

"What? I can just barely hear you," John tried to rise but fell back onto the cot. "I'm dizzy, and my ears are ringing."

"We can't stay here!" Dino shouted. "More shelling is expected, and we need to get back to camp before dark."

"Give me a minute to rest," John said while collapsing back onto the cot.

John and Dino were posing as two Office of Strategic Service (OSS) agents dressed in British fatigues and assigned to the British 70th Infantry Division. They were acting independently under the supervision of the Alsos mission and Colonel Powers. They were to coordinate intelligence-gathering between the Allied forces. Artillery shelling and mortar attacks were not part of their assignment or at least as they understood their mission. They were to record the results of Allied campaigns, watch and report their findings, not become directly involved in the battles.

"It's getting ugly!" Dino shouted to John. "We can't wait for Sergeant Davis; we'll have to contact him later. The Italian Army is attacking from Libya to force the British out of Egypt. Let's get out of here before we get shot."

"But Sergeant Davis has our supplies. What about our food?" John pleaded.

"We'll radio Alsos Headquarters to report our problem."

Dino did not expect John to hear or understand. "We can change our contact point to the Alexandria airport tomorrow afternoon."

As Dino drove away from the bunker, John sank into his seat and quickly fell asleep despite the rough ride. The rumble of artillery fire was fading in the background as the two Alsos agents drove south toward their campsite in the Egyptian desert. Dino thought out loud, "What the hell are we doing here?"

Chapter 8

THE DEPRESSION CAMP

It was as safe and secure a base camp you could find in an active war zone. The fighting was miles away. The location allowed access to many of the roads used by Axis or enemy troops and could be easily accessed from the Qattara Depression, 150 miles southwest of Alexandria. 2,000 miles of sand between Egypt and Morocco made for a miserable battle field and sometimes impossible to locate except by radio communications or following the smoke columns. Little fighting extended deeper than 50 miles.

The base camp of team 2 consisted of a camouflaged tent, two jeeps, and a trailer. The depression provided good ground cover and protection from the many dust storms that popped up quickly. The camp provided great cover from the prying eyes of roving German and Italian patrols. No one in their right mind would venture into such a place, not even the numerous radio trackers and patrols.

Two hours passed before John's hearing returned close to normal. The two old friends returned to their usual banter about anything that appeared to be war, which gave them something to complain about, especially John and his distaste for conflict.

"Colonel Powers said that we would not be in danger on this assignment," John argued with Dino. "It's supposed to be a safe place. Just a slight miscalculation that almost got us killed. Although we were not supposed to be in that British bunker as the Italian force approached." Dino could not argue the point.

"Speaking of Powers, we should report in and send our supply list," John said while nursing his forehead and nose. "You will need to talk to him, I still can't hear well. I'll fix dinner while you send the messages, and I will take your place tomorrow night."

"What fixing? Open two cans and hand me a spoon, but don't put yourself out too much," Dino responded sarcastically.

John's hearing had not completely returned to normal and asked. "Open a spoon for two mush. What does that mean?"

"No, no." Dino said. "Forget it. You just sit there and be quiet until your hearing returns. Besides your cooking or can opening leaves much to be desired."

"Say what?" John countered as he rose from his cot to be closer to Dino to hear the conversation.

"Sit, sit!" Dino shouted as John fell back to the cot. "Take care of your nose and forehead while I talk to Powers."

John finally understood Dino and returned to his seat on the cot. "Don't forget to move the transmitter after each transmission to confuse the Germans trying to find you and the radio by triangulation."

"Yes, mother," Dino responded. "Don't let my dinner get cold while I'm out."

"You are out cold?" John asked in confusion.

"Shut-up and go to sleep." Dino said louder and moved away from the camp.

*　　*　　*

Dino uncovered the jeep and trailer before driving 2 miles through sand and light brush. Driving in the dark was tricky, but he could navigate through the dark with the light of the crescent moon aided by shaded fog lights on the jeep. He drove over several tank tracks and finally chose one of the hard sand roads to begin his transmission to headquarters.

As he keyed his radio under the light of a small flashlight, the transmission came alive. "Eyeball, this is Glacier, over," Dino said into his microphone. Static followed. His directions were to wait seventy seconds and rekey the radio. After seventy seconds, he repeated the call signal. "Eyeball, this is Glacier, over," After a few seconds, the static cleared, and he repeated the recipe for southern bread pudding with Wild Turkey whiskey and cinnamon sauce.

Dino completed the message and gathered the radio and recipe to move to another location 4 miles across the desert to another deserted stretch of road the Germans used during daylight hours. He rekeyed his microphone and repeated the recipe with different ingredients and measurements.

"Eyeball, this is Glacier, over," He had to read the changes quickly. Exactly ninety seconds later, the transmission ended. Silence replaced the static as Alsos Headquarters received the transmission.

Dino marveled at the recipe he had just sent. The original recipe broadcast earlier came from the memoirs of a Confederate soldier published in 1880. The title of the book was *Mississippi Magnolia Trees* and contained the soldiers' favorite bread pudding recipe that his mother made in Jackson, Mississippi. The second transmission with changes contained the coded message to Alsos Headquarters. Both transmissions were different, and the key to decoding the message was to refer to the original recipe.

There were five copies printed of the original manuscript and recipe, most of which remained in the hands of Colonel Powers relatives. Unfortunately, the original manuscript disappeared while at the publisher. A fire had destroyed the publisher's building in 1910, and Powers assumed the manuscript had perished in the fire. Colonel Powers had a copy from his family library, and he felt sure that copies would not appear or used by the Germans to decode Allied messages. The coded message and key should be secure according to Powers and provided a copy for each Alsos team to relay messages to and from headquarters.

It was a cloudless and chilly night. There was a cool breeze formed by the declining evening temperatures typical of high deserts. The crescent moon provided enough light to reveal several dust devils in the distance. Dino was on high alert to possible enemy traffic on the road, and he could easily see a mile or more in each direction, but he was still wary. He did relax enough to smoke one of his favorite Lucky Strike cigarettes and waited the necessary five minutes for a return radio transmission before returning to base camp.

Suddenly, a truck was heading toward his position at a fast speed. He quickly packed the radio, maps, and recipe and drove off into the brush at a 90-degree angle to the road to remain unseen by the truck.

Although the darkness and rough ground slowed his trip, Dino returned safely to the base camp unobserved by the enemy vehicle. It was a large six-wheeled truck speeding toward the coast for more supplies needed by the advancing German Army. A smaller truck approached the spot on the road where Dino had just relayed his message. The Germans had succeeded in following his radio transmission and responded to his location to destroy the radio. He was lucky to have seen the truck coming in time to move off the road. It was no secret now that an Allied radio was in use in the area.

As Dino entered the base camp, he could smell the chili. "I'm glad you are feeling better. I couldn't send the two messages to headquarters and came close to being seen by a fast-moving patrol, but I was able to send one."

"What's for dinner?" Dino asked.

"Cold can of chili. No fires remember," John responded. "I also saved you a couple of cookies, and yes, I have regained much of my hearing. Thanks for not asking," John said. "Did you cover the jeep and trailer well enough to hide them from enemy patrols?"

"Yes, mother!" Dino responded in frustration. "You could have at least prepared something for me. It's your turn tomorrow night to send and receive messages. I did your turn tonight because you are hurt and I'm a nice guy. See if I do you any favors in the future. The maps and recipe are in the jeep with the radio for your use tomorrow night."

"Give me a break, I'm hurt," John said while puffing on an old cigar butt, he found hidden in his coat pocket. "Want another cookie?"

Chapter 9

THE SERGEANTS KIDNAPPED

Sergeants Martinez and Davis were not happy. "What did your orders say about London?" Davis asked.

Neither sergeant had any information about their new posting. They sat uncomfortably outside the briefing room waiting for the briefing to begin. "My orders said to report to this briefing room at 0800 hours. It doesn't say to whom I am to report or why," Martinez added. "Just glad we arrived early and ran into Nate and Blake and the colonel again. Got some breakfast too."

At 0810 hours, the door flung open to the conference room. "Attention, gentlemen." a gruff-speaking master sergeant Douglas announced as he approached the two sergeants followed by Colonel Powers.

"At ease," the colonel said while taking a seat across the table from the two recruits to the Alsos mission. "Good to see you again," Colonel Powers said while shaking the hands of the two sergeants and pausing until the master sergeant had left the room and closed the door. "I hope you don't mind my kidnapping you for a little job in the Mediterranean. You should love your new posting and the countries involved. You will be working again with Nate, Blake, John, and Dino and several different resistance operatives. Sort of a reunion."

The two sergeants had remained quiet until Powers paused. "I thought you had taken a job in Washington and the war was over for you." Martinez said. "For sure, I thought the war was over for me."

"Kidnapped, just like you," Powers added. "Our conversation in this room is to stay in this room. More classified operations and you could die as saboteurs if caught. The OSS has asked for our help in the Mediterranean to devise strategic missions to help end the German advance into other areas in North Africa. It will be more dangerous than past assignments. You will work independently of any Allied forces and wear civilian clothes and, at other times, as soldiers in the British Army. Either side of the war might shoot you. Any questions?"

"Sergeant Davis, you will join John and Dino in the eastern zone of the Mediterranean, while Sergeant Martinez will work closely with Nate and Blake in the western zone." Colonel Powers paused. "You will parachute into the water off the beaches of each of your assigned zones in the early morning. You will join your assigned teams on the beach and prepare secure locations within easy access to the beaches where you will begin Operation Town Square.

"This ends our meeting. The information you have and for your safety, other details of your assignments will be sent to you by encrypted messages. Brush up on your encryption and radio skills. You will receive further details as they are developed. Tomorrow night, you will fly over the drop zone at 3,000 feet with your equipment tethered to your foot into water off the beach to prevent local observation. Should be safe enough."

"Sir, I have a question." Sergeant Grant responded.

"What does 'drop into the water' mean exactly?"

"By parachute from three thousand feet or less," Colonel Powers answered. "From low altitude to avoid accidentally dropping you on the beach or a building. Anything higher would be dangerous."

"Sir, wouldn't it be dangerous if the water was over our heads?"

"You will be equipped with flotation devices, and an OSS Officer will help you out of the water. You afraid of a little water?" Colonel Powers quipped. "Thank you, gentlemen. Good luck, and I will be eagerly awaiting your first messages from your outposts." The colonel left the room with the two sergeants standing at attention, still concerned for their safety.

"I guess the colonel thinks a jump from a perfectly good airplane at three thousand feet in the dark water of unknown depth is safe," Martinez said while sharing a laugh with Davis, still with unanswered questions. "Sounds like fun to me."

Chapter 10

OPERATION TOWNSEND

"What are we supposed to do here?" Martinez asked while driving the old truck. "Colonel Powers was no help in describing what we were going to do in the desert and all this sand. I guess he told you guys."

"You are to cook, wash the dishes, and keep us supplied with cold beer and hot women." Nate answered while jabbing Martinez in the ribs.

"Hope you gringos like frijoles and Carta Blanca. That's all I know how to cook." Martinez answered while rubbing his injured ribs.

"I know what frijoles are, but what is Carta Blanca, a Mexican sandwich?" Nate responded while keeping an eye on the road for tank tracks.

"No, it's a great Mexican beer that will be hard to find out here in the desert."

Blake got tired of the silly banter between the two men as they neared the lava field. "It's time to get serious. We have important work to do in a short time. We must not be seen by any of the Axis forces while we work. We will have to keep quiet and invisible while working in the area."

"How much cover do we have to hide the truck?" Blake asked.

"Don't worry, I have disguised our camp well in the black lava and native green and brown grasses. The truck just appears as a deserted relic left in the desert by the wandering Bedouins but also covered with netting and native grasses." Martinez said while dodging the low outcroppings of lava.

"After we unpack and empty the truck, we can go over the plans that Powers gave us." Blake said.

"I sure would like some of that coffee we brought with us," Blake said while repositioning to ease the pain in his back caused by the hard boards in the back of the truck. "I can tell you the Allies are facing a new and better-prepared enemy since the Desert Fox has taken command of the Axis forces in North Africa. Most of our work is to slow or stop the enemy tanks and trucks."

"I can also tell you that we are to view and record the results of Allied tactics following the battles," Blake continued. "We are to watch only and stay out of active battles. I don't want to have to bury either of you two. We must be careful and invisible to Axis forces. That pretty much covers the plan for Operation Townsend."

After a cup of hot coffee, a Lucky Strike, and a delightful dinner of K-rations served with an extra helping of sand, the three men gathered around the lantern to examine aerial photographs of the area. "Our location in the lava field is ideal because of its closeness to targeted tank paths leading into the desert. Blake continued. We also have several OSS interviews of captured Italian soldiers marking locations of roads and supply depots used by the Axis forces."

"What is so important about this desert?" Martinez asked. "Why do the Germans and Italians want to take it from the British and French?"

"It isn't this desert, but if they can take Egypt, then they control the oil and commercial traffic through the Suez Canal." Nate answered. "The Mediterranean Sea would give the Axis forces access to not only the Arabian oil but also the Baltic Sea oil. Without which, Germany would have a hard time finding enough oil to continue the war here and in Europe."

Then Nate turned to Martinez, the appointed cook. "That wasn't much of a dinner tonight. What have you planned for dinner tomorrow evening?"

34

"Whatever you brought with you. I've eaten all the steaks already, and the soufflé I cooked fell this morning. I suppose you will have to settle for K-rations."

"Not K-rations again," Nate complained.

"Sorry, our kitchen lacks elegance like your restaurants in Socorro," Martinez answered sarcastically.

Blake had to interrupt the two bantering friends again to explain part of the plans for tomorrow evening," As the three men studies the maps Blake continued. "We can start placing the mines and camel dung covers in either of these two tank trails as traffic dies down this evening."

"Those things are disgusting," Nate said. "Why can't we just place mines on the tracks without those covers? They smell as bad as the real camel dung."

"How did we get involved with the covers?" Martinez asked.

"Not sure how, but the colonel ordered them at a suggestion from John and Dino." Nate responded.

"We should place the covers and mines on all available tank trails at the same time to keep the communications between the tanks to a minimum. One of the damaged tanks could alert the other tanks to avoid hitting the mines. The only way the mines can be useful is surprise, and then there may be a few trucks that hit the mines with similar results." Martinez said.

"That may not be an issue if we can get our new gadget working," Nate said. "Alsos Headquarters has built a 'jamming' radio that can interrupt communications between the tanks and command radios. It has a limited range for now but may prevent alerts between tanks and commanders."

"It's still early. We could place some of the mines and covers tonight and try our 'jamming' radio in the morning as the first tanks appear." Martinez added.

"Okay," Blake added. "Let's get a couple of hours of rest and begin at 2000 hours. I'll take the first watch and wake up Nate at 2200 hours. Martinez can take the next watch at 2400 hours. We can start placing mines at 0100. Now get some rest."

Chapter 11

THE DEPRESSION

John and Dino made their way to the Alexandria airport to meet a British agent named Captain Huffington. They met at the main entrance, made introductions and immediately left in a British patrol lorry to recover the much-needed supplies and Sergeant Davis. Davis was to arrive shortly to bring the cargo from Alsos Headquarters and join the Alsos team in the depression.

The dark green British military version of the DC-3 aircraft rolled to a stop in front of a small warehouse away from the main terminal as the two Also operatives and the British agent approached.

John and Dino, with Captain Huffington of British Intelligence, stopped at the warehouse and patiently waited for Sergeant Davis and the cargo to be unloaded.

"Did you have any trouble getting to the airport?" Captain Huffington asked. "The city is on alert to another attack by the Axis forces."

"No trouble in the city, but we did see several German transports unloading equipment and troops further north, probably just across the Libyan border," Dino answered. "It's obvious the Italian troops and accompanying German advisers are preparing for an attack."

"We have provided this warehouse for your use, but I would suggest you take everything you need quickly," Captain Huffington said. "Your jeep and trailer are parked in the warehouse, and you should load as much of your supplies as possible today. A possible attack over the border may limit your future access to the airport."

"Thank you, Captain. We'll leave as soon as possible," John said while shaking his hand. "We'll stay in contact with you as needed. You know where we will be, at least for now. Any supplies we can't take now we will pick-up later."

After a halfhearted salute, Captain Huffington drove off quickly, leaving John and Dino waiting for Sergeant Davis.

"Where is Davis?" Dino asked. "We need to leave as soon as possible."

As if magic, Sergeant Davis appeared at the doorway as the plane's engines finally shut down. "Did you bring our mine covers and the other supplies we need?" John asked before Davis could reach the ground.

"Yes, Colonel Powers was insistent that you needed them before I left headquarters. What do you plan to do with this stuff?" Davis asked.

"You will see tonight as we place them on two of the tank tracks the Germans use as they advance into the desert," Dino responded. "Did you bring the other items we needed?"

"Yes, I did but reluctantly," Davis answered. "You must be crazy to try to use poison sumac on Axis troops. It is lethal, even though the Geneva Convention does not recognize it."

"We don't plan to use it where it could be lethal," John answered. "It could save lives of those exposed. The scratching and discomfort will influence their willingness to fight. They could die only if they breathe the fumes. Otherwise, they will just itch and scratch and wish they were someplace else."

Davis continued to question its use. "What about Allied forces? Won't they come in contact with the sumac?"

"We plan to map and define the areas exposed for the Allied troops, much like a minefield. If they touch the sumac, they should wash the exposed area with cold water within ten minutes to halt any potential skin exposure," John answered. "That's the reason for the aerosol—to spray the native grasses inside Axis troop movement areas."

"I remember, as a kid, touching poison sumac. I couldn't get rid of it until my mother bathed me in cold water and trashed my favorite jeans and wool shirt. She then put something like oatmeal on the whelps to stop the itching." Davis said.

"How will we spray the native grasses without exposing ourselves?"

"Carefully," Dino said. "We will need a windless day and wear a gas mask in case some of the spray drifts toward us. It will be dangerous, but the results could save many lives. We will have a similar problem with applying the mines and camel dung covers, possibly blown to pieces or discovered by the Axis forces and shot. We need to be careful. Quick installation and disappear."

"Our eventual goal is to slow the Axis forces to save Allied lives," John added. "Let's get out of here, we need to make the depression before dark. Our Bedouin neighbors don't like strangers, especially at night. It is about 150 miles of mainly desert roads between the airport and the depression."

The supply loading was complete as the team headed out of the airport toward the depression. A short distance out of the airport, Dino had a question for Sergeant Davis. "What do you think of the mine covers?"

"Crazy, but I think they might work. Colonel Powers was skeptical. Lieutenant Townsend was hysterical, and Sergeant Jackson was still laughing as I left."

"It might work and slow the progress of a few tanks into battle," Davis answered. "The sumac is still of concern. It seems that it would affect Allied and Axis forces alike, and I can't imagine how the foot soldiers would respond once in contact with the sumac. They may itch and scratch, but won't they continue to fight?"

"Probably," Dino answered with a grin. "They will itch and scratch for several days following the fighting. They will move and think slowly and avoid moving. They will do anything to relieve the pain and itching. More interested in relief than fighting."

"Don't you think the commanders are prepared for contact with sumac?" Davis asked, still not convinced. "What about a cream to stop the itching? Their doctors must be prepared too?"

"Fortunately for us, few doctors are available to the troops. Most of the Italian doctors stay on the mainland and not available," John added while checking the time. "We must stay in Alexandria tonight. It is too late to wander into the desert and approach the depression and the Bedouin encampment."

"Where can we stay?" Davis asked.

"Huffington mentioned a safe house used by British Intelligence and OSS if we should need it. Stay here tonight and leave early tomorrow to arrive at the depression midmorning," Dino explained. "The trip in sunlight will give us the chance to find any German fuel tanks and pipelines. More targets for the Alsos teams."

"I hope we find the safe house soon. I'm starving and need a drink," Davis said while studying a map of the city. "Where is it exactly?"

"I have an address, but I've never been there," Dino said while sharing the map with Davis. "The address is 239 Piccadilly Square. Should be coming up on the right in about fifteen blocks. You can sure see the British influence in this country. Makes you wonder how many more Piccadilly Squares there are in the world. Probably everywhere the British have set up political and trading relations," Dino voiced his opinion. "Probably won't see many Jones, Oak, or Pecan streets here, not much American influence seen here."

"Turn right at the next street." Davis advised. "Should be the small white house on the right, number 239. We will need to change into typical British clothing and hide the jeep and trailer."

"We should change before we venture out onto the streets. There are not supposed to be any American soldiers in Alexandria," John advised. "You will look great in your new robe, but we can't wear the Bedouin stuff until we leave Alexandria. The British shorts and shirt will be best here with open collar for comfort."

Chapter 12

The Sand Trap

Erwin Rommel was pushing the British troops deeper into the desert, much to their dismay. The squad leader of British B114 East was tired of retreating and faced with more of the same when a young private named Aaronson came into his tent.

Out of frustration, Sergeant Blackford agreed to listen to the private. "What is it, Aaronson?"

"In 1936, my family and I were taking a holiday in Egypt when a windstorm suddenly forced us off the road into a ditch, where we took refuge in our two Land Cruisers until the storm ended. Digging out of the loose sand was almost impossible. Move one shovel full and another would fall into its place. The storm created large pools of loose sand almost like quicksand minus the water. More like baking powder and covered everything. Even with four-wheel-drive vehicles, it was impossible to get our Land Cruisers out of the sand. We had to dig ourselves out of the powder."

"That's real interesting, Aaronson, but what does that have to do with us?" Sergeant Blackford asked.

"Our four-wheel-drive vehicles sank into the sand up to the axles, making escape difficult," Aaronson explained. "I spotted several of those loose sand pools along the road that we could use to direct the tanks to stop them in their tracks."

"There is no way the German tank commanders would fall for a trick like that. They are smart and moving fast, unafraid of any opposition."

Aaronson interrupted the sergeant by telling him. "It's the speed and that they are unafraid of opposition that make them vulnerable to such a trick."

"It might be worth a try," Blackford responded. "Ask Corporal Biggs to come to my tent."

Aaronson was pleasantly surprised the sergeant would try the trick. Without answering the sergeant, he ran out of the squad leader's tent in search of Biggs.

"Corporal Biggs, the sergeant wants to see you." Aaronson explained as he ran into Biggs's tent.

"Okay. Okay," Biggs answered. "I'll be right there as soon as I finish my letter."

"I think the sergeant means now. He wants to talk to you about a trick to stop the advancing German tanks."

"Let me put on my boots, and I'll be right there," Biggs told the private. "I can't believe this can't wait until tomorrow morning."

Biggs and Aaronson finally joined the sergeant in his tent, where he was examining a recent photograph and a map of German and Italian tank routes. "What did you want, Sergeant?"

"I'm not sure, but I want you to hear what Aaronson is proposing to stop some of the German and Italian tanks."

Aaronson explained his plan again and left the two men to discuss the possibility to put the plan to a test. A short time later, Blackford and Biggs rousted the squad out of their sleep for a quick briefing. "Take a knee, gentlemen. Smoke, if you have them. Tomorrow at 0300 hours, we are going to disable some tanks. We are going to create two detours into soft sand pools that will swallow the tanks, making them useless. If you think it sounds crazy, it probably is, but if it works, it will slow the Axis advance and perhaps save some lives."

"I have a question?" one of the squad members responded. "The tank crews will leave their tanks if they are stuck in the sand to find another tank, either to pull them out of the sand or join other tank crews. Won't they just advance in another tank?"

"Yes, that is when we can place some sugar, mothballs, or soap into their fuel tanks that will destroy their engines." Blackford explained.

Biggs added. "The average life of the engines in most tanks is about three hundred hours. We can reduce that number to about one hundred hours by using the mothballs, sugar, or soap, even fewer hours if you consider the wear caused by sand."

A bewildered squad member raised a question. "Where will we find enough soap, sugar, or mothballs to disable fifty or more tanks?"

"And how will we place that stuff in the tanks stuck in the sand without being shot?"

"Won't the German troops be alerted to our location?"

"Not if we cover our tracks and move our camp out of sight," Corporal Biggs explained. "I will find the soap and sugar, and if you have time, there will be plenty of sand to add to the tanks. As the other tanks move around the tanks in the sand, we will place the soap and sugar in the abandoned tanks. If they leave a watch over the tanks, we will dispose of him quietly and move away from the site before replacement troops can respond."

Another question was forming in Aaronson's mind, but he decided to keep silent. He wondered why mothballs or soap would stop a tank engine. He knew that sugar clogged fuel filters and injectors, but he was not familiar with the effect soap or mothballs would have on the engines.

"If that is all, get some sleep. We will begin at 0300 hours." Sergeant Blackford announced and dismissed the squad.

Biggs suggested alerting field headquarters as the squad was filing out of the briefing. "Alert them of our mission to keep us out of trouble." Blackford ordered.

Biggs radioed a simple message to headquarters and then went to bed.

Within minutes, the radio came to life. "Equator 2, this is North Pole, over." It was a simple unencrypted message.

"What the hell are you doing?" North Pole asked.

"North Pole, this is Equator 2, over," Biggs answered while trying to think of a good excuse for their mission. "Just a short field trip and we will be back and available for action as needed by 0700 hours."

"Sounds crazy. I hope it works. Keep it short and let us know what happens." Headquarters signed off as the radio went silent.

*   *   *

The light of the half-moon shone on the roads in the desert at 0300 hours as the mission began. The plan was taking shape quickly, and the whole squad worked feverishly to finish the detours before sunrise.

The detour began with several attempts to design a suitable black and white sign pointing toward the sand trap. "Anyone know how to spell 'detour'?"

"D-T-O-U-R," someone answered.

"No, no, no. I mean, in German, and you misspelled 'detour.' There is an E after the D." There were no volunteers with the correct spelling of the word in German.

"I know the German word for 'attention,'" One of the squad members answered. "I know the word but don't know how to spell that either."

"Forget it. I'll make the arrow bigger with no word. That will have to do." Biggs said in frustration.

The soft sand was about 50 yards off the road. It was hoped that several tanks would amass behind the first tanks as they sank in the sand. "I hope we can ensnare several tanks before the following tanks notice." Aaronson said.

Aaronson was working alongside Blackford and decided to ask the question he had but didn't voice during the briefing. "What effect does soap and mothballs have on the diesel engines of the tanks?"

"Sugar and mothballs fowl the fuel filters and injectors of most engines. However, the mothballs react differently in diesel engines. At first, the engine performs better as the mothballs increase the octane rating of the fuel and results in better gas mileage. Over time, the increased heat produced by burning higher octane fuel will fuse the pistons to the piston walls, or the increased temperature can blow the head gaskets and possibly start a fire within the tank."

Aaronson answered. "It doesn't happen immediately but over time. I suppose that will allow anyone placing the sugar or soap in the fuel to escape undetected."

"The tanks are coming! Let's get out of here," Corporal Biggs shouted as the squad scrambled into the lorry and drove away from the sand trap. "Let's pick a spot out of sight to watch what happens."

Chapter 13

Dino Requests Camel Dung

"Sergeant Jackson, we just received a message from John and Dino," The radio operator sounded confused as he passed the message to the sergeant. "The deciphered message doesn't make sense. They are asking us to design and make an exploding camel turd."

"A what?" Jackson asked. "You must have misread the message. We work with a lot with turds around here but not any that explode," The sergeant took the message from the radio operator and began reading the deciphered message. "I think I better give this to the head turd around here, it may have some significance to him, but I bet it's a joke." The sergeant grinned as he took the message down the hall to Colonel Powers.

Sergeant Jackson knocked on the open door to the colonel's office and quietly laid the message down on a small pile of notes on his desk. "Sir, you may want to see this message just received from John and Dino. We may have misinterpreted the message, but perhaps you know something about their request."

Colonel Powers turned back to his desk from the map on the wall he was studying to see the sergeant grinning like a Cheshire Cat. "What's so funny?" Without waiting for an answer, the colonel picked up the message and burst out laughing. "You didn't misunderstand the message—they are wanting a cover for the land mines to appear like camel dung. The normal land mines have not performed well in the sand. If buried deep enough to hide them, the tanks run over them without detonating. If they bury the mines shallow enough to detonate in the sand, the tank drivers see them and drive around them. John and Dino want to have a cover designed as camel dung to disguise them."

The surprised Sergeant Jackson was amused but perplexed, trying hard not to laugh at the colonel's explanation. "Why disguise the mines as camel dung?"

"Dino discovered the tank drivers were purposely hitting the piles of camel dung in hopes of splashing the foot soldiers or flinging dung behind them to hit one of the following tank drivers. This disguise will either stop some tanks or some of the soldiers who have been collecting the dung for evening fires," Colonel Powers tried to keep a straight face while thinking of other reasons. "I suppose the soldiers who have experienced the splashing dung will appreciate our artificial dung pile, except that it will explode instead of just smelling bad."

"Will you take this request to the Office of Strategic Services technicians? They will laugh me out of the building."

Powers agreed with the sergeant and left for the OSS building next door. They wouldn't laugh at the request made by a colonel, at least not to his face. The technicians were great artisans with wood and metals but little experience with more malleable materials soft enough to form something to appear as camel dung. He first thought of latex, but latex was difficult to find during the war. Possibly one of the new plastics developed by BASF or Durite Plastics would work, but most plastics were hard and brittle.

The staff sergeant on duty at the OSS office stood and saluted as Colonel Powers approached his desk. "At ease, Sergeant," Powers returned the salute. "I need to speak to your technicians about a weapon to disable German tanks."

"Yes, sir, follow me."

Powers followed the sergeant down the hall and down two flights of stairs into the bowels of the two-story building. This was the headquarters group of skilled machinists and technical specialists charged with developing weapons to stop the enemy. Their skills were unquestioned by everyone in the army, earning them the title of "crazy scientists."

"Colonel Powers, this is Lieutenant Townsend, director of the laboratory." After the sergeant introduced the two men, he turned, and left them to discuss Power's needs.

"Captain Townsend, good to see you again." Powers said.

"Thank you, sir. It's good to see you again. I hope you have forgotten the 'train wreck' I caused in Hawaii," He was referring to his slow actions on a shipment of needed supplies for a Korean village and to extract an Alsos team for the mission ahead of the advancing Russian troops in North Korea. "Seems like years since we last met."

"Sergeant Blair tells me your performance since that day has been excellent," Powers replied. "Chalk it up to experience for a new officer." Powers continued before explaining his request.

"Yes, Sergeant Blair was close to executing me on your orders. He scarred the hell out of me."

"I'm glad we didn't ruin your career or have you executed. Would have been a terrible waist of good man-power," Powers continued. "Seems your career has taken an upward trend now as director of this great laboratory. I need your help now. I have a project that will be different from most of your work. I need a device to stop German tanks in the North Africa campaign." Powers described the project and asked when he could have fifty units ready for delivery.

Townsend was having trouble controlling his smile and laughter but assured the colonel the project could be completed in thirty days.

"You have a week, Captain," Colonel Powers said. "And make sure they are soft enough to appear like the real thing," As he turned to leave, Powers turned back to Townsend. "We were kidding about having you shot in Hawaii."

"I hoped so, sir. Sergeant Blair had me convinced that you would have me court-martialed and shot if I didn't improve," Townsend answered. "It did scare the hell out of me, and my performance improved daily, following your rebuke. I'm a much better officer because of you. Thank you, sir."

Chapter 14

SET THE TRAPS

"Up and at 'em," Blake announced to the two men trying to sleep. The team had needed the rest after the long trip and the extensive planning needed to place the camel dung covers over the mines. It was 0200 hours when Blake awakened the team to begin placing the mines. "We must finish the job before the tank traffic begins."

Martinez was responsible for digging the holes, while Nate placed the mines in the sand. It was Blake's responsibility to position the dung covers.

"If all goes as planned, the German tank drivers will steer for the camel dung to splash the foot soldiers or the driver of the following tank." Blake explained.

"You give deception a bad name. These covers are nasty. They even smell like dung." Martinez added.

"Not my idea. John and Dino had them designed and produced." Nate said while placing another mine in the sand.

"Hurry up, you guys!" Blake said. "We need to finish burying and covering all the mines before dawn. We don't want to be found placing these in the tracks."

"I found a perfect place for us to hide and watch the fireworks," Nate said. "It's a rocky outcropping about 300 yards from the minefield and should give us good cover and out of sight. We can park the lorry on the downslope of the hill and well hidden from view."

"That will have to do for tonight." Blake said as the first pink rays of the sunrise were beginning to form on the eastern horizon.

"We should move to the hiding place Nate found before traffic starts moving westward into the desert," Blake advised. "Let's get out of here."

Chapter 15

DIRTY TRICKS

"We just received a request for more help from one of your teams." Captain Townsend said as he entered Colonel Powers' office.

The colonel sat at his desk, trying to relax following a telephone call from British headquarters accusing his teams of dirty tricks. There were inflammatory remarks directed at the independent efforts of his teams. "They will get over it." Colonel Powers said as he turned to meet Captain Townsend.

"This request involves moving team 2 from their current position in the Libyan Desert to Malta to work with the Italian resistance." Townsend said.

"Wonderful! All we need is more team movements." Powers answered.

"The request stated the new location would need to be Malta rather than Sicily, where they would begin work with the Italian resistance." Townsend replied. "Another OSS agent will contact you tomorrow to discuss the arrangements and answer your questions. Where do you want to meet the agent?"

"Not here, there are unfriendly eyes and ears everywhere. He shouldn't come to our office," Powers said. "There is a pub three blocks south of here called 'The Hunter'. We can meet there at 1430 hours. I'll be in civvies and wearing a red Boston Red Sox cap."

"I'll tell the agent." Townsend said as he turned to leave Powers' office.

"How will I recognize him?" Powers asked.

"You won't. He'll find you and ask for the time." Townsend added.

Colonel Powers knew that John and Dino would welcome the change in locations and the chance to work again with the Italian underground. He would wait until after the meeting with the OSS agent to tell John and Dino. Sergeant Davis was to keep them out of trouble and away from active fighting. This assignment would be more dangerous.

John mentioned during the first meeting with Colonel Powers that he would like to work with the Italian underground again, especially Nora, the beautiful leader of the local underground in Genoa. He may not be as eager to work with strangers like the new OSS agent assigned to help them in Malta.

Their work together in Genoa produced two important physicists who agreed to join the efforts of the Manhattan Project in building the atomic bomb. The German High Command also wanted the two physicists and held them captive until they would be of help to Heisenberg in Hechinger, Germany. Their expertise was to create a radioactive pile that could go critical, a necessary ingredient in building an atomic bomb.

The radio operator suddenly interrupted Powers and Townsend. He was frantically describing the radio message from team 2 in Libya.

"Slow down, corporal. Tell me what's wrong." Powers said while motioning for the corporal to take a seat.

"It is team 2 in Libya, sir. I made the usual early-morning contact with them, but there was no response. I am worried but did not report the missed contact. I decided to try again, but there was no response. They are not responding to their radio."

"When did you last hear from them?" Powers asked.

"It was last week at the appointed day and time," the corporal answered. "We take supply calls from them every week."

"Don't panic, corporal, I'm sure there is a good reason they are not responding. They were to start placing the mines and dung covers this week and probably busy. We probably will hear from them soon." Powers said while trying to reassure himself and the corporal.

The OSS Agent

Colonel Powers left early for the meeting with the OSS agent. He picked a booth in the back, near the bathrooms, of the mostly empty Hunter Pub. At exactly 1430 hours, an attractive young woman entered the pub and asked the waiter for directions to the bus station. At the same time, she scanned the pub for her contact.

"May I use your restroom?" the young woman asked. The waiter pointed to the back of the pub without answering.

Instead of taking a seat opposite Powers, the young woman passed his table, showing no interest or eye contact. Powers was sure she was the agent but remained seated, reading his book and picking at his meat pie left by the waiter moments earlier. Something has happened.

Minutes later, the young woman passed by his table while rubbing wet hands together on a paper towel and casually dropped a note on his table. Powers quickly placed the note inside his book without raising his eyes from the book and continued picking at his meat pie.

The young woman left the pub heading in the direction the waiter had pointed out for the bus station. Fifteen minutes later, Powers read the note while seated on a park bench across the street from the bus station.

"I'm seated in the bus station. Make sure no one is following you," the note read.

Powers closed his book containing the note and began scanning the people around him. He walked two blocks away from the bus station, turned into a bookstore, and positioned himself by the door to watch for anyone following. After he felt sure no one was following him, he left the bookstore and headed back toward the bus station.

He stopped several times to scan the faces in the crowd and felt sure there were no prying eyes.

Powers returned to the bus station and stepped inside the door. When he was sure no one was following, he joined the young woman seated on the long wooden bench with many other passengers awaiting various buses.

Without raising her head, she whispered, "Were you followed?"

"I'm sure no one followed me. We are safe," Powers answered.

"That pub is not safe. I have seen German agents there on several occasions and suspect it is a drop location," the young woman said.

"I didn't know, or I would have chosen a meeting place more carefully," Powers said, feeling embarrassed. "I'm not a good spook, am I?"

"You're not supposed to be," the young woman responded. "I have described most of the information you need about the assignment in a handwritten note in the sports section of the newspaper next to you. I will contact you tomorrow for further discussions. Take the paper and go before we draw attention to our conversation."

Powers stood, stuffed the folded paper under his arm as he approached the ticket agent. He asked for direction to the bathroom, paused to check for prying eyes, and went to the restroom. He carefully checked the stalls, found them empty, locked himself in, and read the note. The torn pieces of the note disappeared down the commode after he read them. He felt certain he could recall the message. On his way back to his office, he tossed the paper in the trash outside the bus station doorway.

The office was quiet while Powers concentrated on the note. He was in the process of writing the details on a notepad when the radio operator ran into his office.

"Sir, you have received an urgent message form British headquarters."

"I know, another complaint about camel dung or sand traps." Powers said. "You would think something that works would be of interest to those guys rather than complain about dirty tricks."

"The Mines are Working"

The rocky outcropping provided great cover for the team. It was about 0700 hours when the sun began to rise. The chill in the air persisted as vehicle traffic began to approach the minefield.

Nate asked for a cigarette to calm his nerves, while Blake and Martinez watched the approaching vehicles. "I have a cigar, if you want." Martinez offered while digging in his shirt pocket.

"I need a light." Nate responded in frustration.

"Keep quiet." Blake said as the traffic came closer.

"There are no tanks," Martinez noted while watching the traffic through binoculars. "It's a supply formation headed into the desert. Double deuces with covered backs coming fast."

The first truck made it past the first three rows of dung-covered mines but hit one of the last piles as two following trucks struck the mines. The concussion detonated several other mines as more trucks either stopped in the devastation or remained outside the range of the explosions.

"Six trucks were destroyed, and two others are on fire!" Nate shouted and gave Blake a thumbs-up sign.

Martinez concentrated on the last few trucks in the formation. "Don't relax yet. The last two trucks have stopped. Twenty soldiers are spilling out onto the road and rushing toward the burning trucks."

"One of the truck drivers stopped them from entering the minefield. They could have detonated more of the mines," Nate responded. "I'm surprised the concussion detonated some of the other mines."

"That may continue as the concussion and the fires heat other mines. Seems like a good time for us to leave." Martinez said.

It was surprisingly quiet after the first few mines exploded. The soldiers helped injured truck drivers and the remaining trucks killed their engines. Little could be done for the injured truck drivers, except to load them into front seats with limited space in the back of the remaining trucks. Almost as quickly as it happened, the trucks were turning around to return to the coast.

"We stopped or destroyed a supply truck formation but no tanks." Blake responded.

Unexpectedly, the radio in the truck came alive. "Turkey, this is Hot Water, over. Do you read? Turkey, this Hot Water, over. Come in."

"Shut it off!" Blake whispered as static erupted from the radio. Some of the German soldiers heard the radio sound and began dropping to the sand or moving behind the trucks with weapons pointed at the outcropping.

The three men crawled away from the rock outcropping and toward the old truck still producing static heard by the Germans. Several of the German soldiers began moving toward the sound just as the old lorry came to life and began to move safely into the desert.

It took about five minutes for the advancing German soldiers to reach the rock outcropping to find it deserted, except for a cold cigar butt and a faint trail in the sand made by the old truck. The three men made it safely away from the area before Martinez asked, "Who tried to contact us? They almost got us killed!"

"That was close!" Blake said. "We didn't stop any tanks but did stop about ten supply trucks heading to the front. I wonder if any of the drivers intentionally hit the camel dung or maybe we were just lucky."

"Luck had nothing to do with it," Nate responded. "Those mines would have exploded after the first mine detonated, whether hit by a truck or not."

"Why was our radio left on and receiving?" Martinez asked. "That mistake gave our position away! We could have been shot if captured. The Germans now know we are working in the area, and they will be looking for us."

"It's my fault," Blake said. "I planned to contact headquarters with our weekly supply order and failed to shut it off. We still need to give them our supply order and report on the effectiveness of the mine covers."

"We have one more minefield to place on the other side of the lava field. Pack everything when we reach camp and prepare to move tonight. It's probably wise to avoid contact with the roving Germans patrols, especially since they know we are in the area." Martinez said while studying a map to locate their next base camp.

"I will call headquarters to report our move and stall the next supply order until we have settled into a new location," Blake said. "They're probably concerned that we missed our scheduled contact. Anything look good for our new base camp?"

"We need some shade from the sun and be close to a water source," Martinez answered. "Maybe we should join John and Dino in the depression in Egypt. The Bedouins have provided great cover and are good neighbors. The best part is the Italian or German soldiers don't want any contact with the Bedouins."

"What about water?" Nate asked. "Do they have a good source of water?"

"They are hauling water from Alexandria and adding sterilizing capsules to kill the bacteria," Blake answered. "Tastes funny, but it is safe to drink."

"Should we contact John and Dino before we make a surprise visit to their camp?" Martinez asked. "Especially since the Bedouins distrust all foreigners."

"You radio them and make it quick," Blake said. "We don't want to give away our position."

"Glacier, this is Turkey, come in," Martinez keyed the radio. "Glacier, this is Turkey," Martinez repeated the call.

The static stopped as John keyed the radio. "Turkey, this is Glacier, do you read?"

"Loud and clear, Glacier. Team 1 headed your way, our position compromised. What are your coordinates? ETA is 2100 hours tomorrow. One more minefield must be prepared before we leave."

"Roger, Turkey, over and out."

Chapter 16

Sand Traps Work

Sergeant Blackford ordered everyone into the two lorries and drove away. Biggs felt sure the tanks did not hear the squad leave the area.

"I hope this works. If it stops any of the tanks from moving toward the battle, it has been worth the effort," Biggs said to Aaronson.

"Can't we stop and check the effectiveness of the sand trap?" Aaronson asked.

"Okay. Stop the truck," Biggs ordered. "Let's check with Blackford."

Biggs keyed his radio and asked for permission to stop to take a few pictures.

"We will stay out of sight. Aaronson and I will climb the dune, take a couple of pictures, and be back in a flash," Biggs said.

The sun was up, and the temperature had risen 20 degrees and rising fast. The squad had retreated several hundred yards using the hardpan between the tall sand dunes. "It should be safe for us to leave the trucks here, climb the dune, and take a couple of pictures," Biggs mentioned to Blackford.

"Leave everything in the lorry that might shine or make a sound. Cover your heads to blend with the sand," Blackford ordered.

Biggs and Aaronson climbed the 30-foot tall sand dune carefully. "This is not a place you would want to be in a windstorm," Biggs said.

"I know," Aaronson said. "I was in one. That's what gave me the idea for the sand trap."

The two men approached the crown of the dune on their bellies very quietly. "Stay down until I tell you," Biggs whispered. They were still about 6 feet from the top of the dune. Biggs raised his cloth-covered head enough to see the tanks.

"It worked," Biggs whispered. "Three tanks stopped with sand up to the gun turret, probably spilling sand into the tank through the driver's door. The rest of the tanks are stopped behind them."

"Let me take a couple of pictures," Aaronson said. "The other tanks seem confused. A soldier from the first tank is shouting orders to the other tanks."

"The other tanks are backing out of the sand and stopping on the original tank path," Biggs said. "I can't believe none of the other tanks are helping the tanks stuck in the sand. They seem unwilling to help. Maybe their engines have failed because of the sand."

Aaronson took three pictures with his Voigtlander IIa 35mm camera. He quickly tucked the camera back into his tunic as the two men crept back down the dune. The two men rejoined the squad and safely left the sand trap in the trusty old lorries.

"It worked!" Aaronson said excitedly while climbing into the lorry next to Sergeant Blackford. "I got pictures too."

"How many tanks took the bait?" Blackford asked.

"Three sank in the sand up to their turrets, while the rest of the tanks backed out of the detour and onto the road. They made no effort to help move the tanks out of the sand trap," Biggs answered while taking notes to send to British field headquarters.

"A good day's work," Blackford stated. "Three tanks destroyed and the rest of the tanks either returned to base or continued to the battle site too late to be of help—great job, Private Aaronson."

"I'll brew you a cup of *jildi*, my favorite desert brew," Biggs told Aaronson as they neared their bivouac area. "Two or three lumps?"

"Not before you report to field headquarters. They need to know we are now available and let them know the sand trap idea worked," Blackford added.

Chapter 17

MORE SAND TRAPS

Captain Townsend and Major Duherst of MI6 knocked on the door to Colonel Powers's office.

"Come in," Powers said as the two men entered and stood at attention until Powers asked them to take seats while he finished his call. He ended his phone conversation before addressing the two visitors. "To what do I owe this pleasure?"

The three officers stood as Townsend introduced Duherst. The two senior officers shook hands before returning to their seats.

"Major Duherst has some information you may find interesting," Captain Townsend said before turning the conversation over to Duherst.

"Yes, sir, last week, a diversion was effective in stopping the advance of ten Panzer tanks into a battle with British forces in Libya. It seems that a young private by the name of Aaronson convinced his squad leader to place a detour in the path of a column of tanks into loose and deep sand where several of the tanks sank and were disabled. The balance of the tanks backed out of the detour and returned to their base and never joined the battle. It turned out to be a decisive British victory over unprotected and outgunned Italian and German forces."

"Aaronson should be decorated for his brilliance and taking the initiative in stopping those tanks," Colonel Powers said. "Did Captain Townsend tell you about our simple and sometimes effective tactics in battle? I guess he also told you about the camel dung covers."

"Yes, sir, he did. Sounds crazy, but it worked. I suppose you must be a little disappointed the covers didn't work on the tanks, but I can tell you the destroyed trucks and the supplies did not reach the Italian troops and resulted in the surrender of 4,500 Italian troops who were hungry and out of ammunition. It was a total success."

"When did you stop laughing about our little invention?" Powers finally asked. "You must have had misgivings about the effectiveness of such a simple and smelly diversion."

"I still laugh every time I think about it or repeat the story," Duherst said.

"The team that placed the camel dung-covered mines proposed another diversion that would have been worse," Colonel Powers related. "They were aware that poison sumac was native to the high desert of Libya. The team proposed to burn the sumac and let the wind carry the smoke onto the troops. There would be more scratching than fighting. No real damage done, just uncomfortable. However, it was learned that sumac smoke can blind, or if inhaled, it can be fatal."

"I'm glad they decided against the use of the sumac burn. As a gas, it would be against the Geneva Convention. Since it was smoke rather than a gas, it would have been acceptable under the Geneva Convention," Townsend said.

"I would like to meet Private Aaronson and his sand trap," Powers said. "We could use him to train my teams and others to recognize and use the sand traps throughout North Africa, and I like his deceiving mind."

"Consider it done. The private is now a corporal and showing other squads to recognize and use the traps," Duherst added while shaking Powers hand before leaving.

"Thank you, Major," Powers said. As captain Townsend turned to escort Major Duherst out of the building, Powers asked a question.

"Captain Townsend, do you have time to discuss another matter?"
"Sure." Townsend responded.

Powers closed the door. "It has come my attention that we have lost contact with John and Dino. They were in Malta when we lost them. Would you work with the radio operator to reestablish contact with them? It isn't like them to disappear so quickly."

"Yes, sir," Townsend said while leaving Powers' office. "What time did you lose them? Close to the time they arrived in Malta? Weren't they to meet Maj. Murphy Donnelly? OSS probably had a location and time for Donnelly, I will check with them."

"Thank you, captain." Powers said as the two men parted.

Chapter 18

MOVE TO SICILY

Team 2 in Egypt was ordered to move to Sicily and work with the Italian underground. They were skeptical at first because of the dangerous move to Sicily and the heavily-guarded southern coastal region. A change in the final details was much more acceptable and less dangerous. A shorter submarine trip to Malta would be better.

The details of the move were worked out in the basement freight-receiving area of Alsos Headquarters the day following Powers' meeting with the OSS agent. The agent arrived as planned but was hardly recognizable dressed in freight-delivery overalls. Her unusual disguise made her entry into Alsos Headquarters inconspicuous and unobserved by prying eyes. Following the meeting, Powers immediately issued the sketchy plan for the team's move, not a perfect plan but workable.

The radio operator sending the plan to the team appeared concerned about the details and approached Powers. "Sir, this plan won't work if the team is late for the pickup on the beach. If they miss the British submarine, they will have to wait two days for another. That's assuming the German and Italian submarines in the area allow it to pass through Gibraltar."

"What do you think we should change in the plans?" Powers asked.

"Why not have the team fly to Malta aboard an Italian aircraft in civilian attire headed for Sicily? That way, they could avoid the German submarines roaming the Mediterranean."

"That's a great idea, corporal. They could fly out of Alexandria bound for Malta much safer and quicker than a long underwater trip in a submarine as we originally planned. The team can easily disguise themselves as Italian newspaper journalists reporting to the large newspaper that they used before while working in Genoa. That will save several days underwater and much safer." Powers said as he changed the plans originally broadcast to the team.

"What should I tell the Italian underground?" the radio operator asked. "They are expecting to pick up team 2 off the coast of Southern Sicily in six days."

"Have the Italians meet team 2 off the coast of Malta instead," Colonel Powers ordered. "Saves time for everyone and much safer."

"Shall I cancel the original orders and issue the new orders, sir?"

"Yes, and tell British headquarters there is no need for the submarine."

Team 2 Leaves Egypt

John and Dino were awaiting orders from Alsos Headquarters after finally placing the rest of the dung-covered mines in two more tank tract areas. Their job done, they looked forward to another assignment. There were fourteen tanks destroyed and, more importantly, several battles fought and won by the British engaging German and Italian troops unsupported by the missing tanks.

"I will miss this place," John said while emptying the sand out of his left boot. "I enjoy the solitude, the cool nights, and the thousands of stars visible in the desert sky."

"What about the snakes and scorpions?" Dino asked. "Aren't you going to miss them too?"

"No, nor will I miss placing the camel dung covers over the land mines. I know we were successful in stopping several tanks and perhaps saving many lives, but I would rather leave the sand here. I haven't had a meal since we arrived here that wasn't laced with sand."

"Do you think we will work with the same Italian underground as before in Genoa?" Dino asked in hopes of some reassurance that he would see Nora again.

"It's unlikely this far south, but as we move north toward Rome and Genoa, we will meet her again. What was the name of the old man we found in Genoa and barrowed his old Renault?" John said.

"I don't remember his name or Nora's assistant's either. We must remember their names before we move further north in Italy. They will be important contacts as we move north," Dino responded. "What about Blake and Nate?" Dino asked. "They were to join us in the depression tomorrow. Hope headquarters has changed their plans too. How are we going to find Italian clothing for the trip to Malta and Sicily? I'll need several cameras if I am to pose as a photographer," Dino said.

"You heard the same instruction I did—everything will be ready for us at the airport in Alexandria. I hope the cameras will be there too," John answered but sounding concerned.

"What are we supposed to do with the jeep and trailer?" Dino asked. "I guess that OSS agent we meet at the airport will find a way to dispose of them."

"I'm planning to drive the jeep to the airport, leave it in the parking area, and leave the trailer here in the depression. If the OSS agent doesn't pick it up, the Bedouins will take it," John answered. "They have been good neighbors. They could use a good trailer to tow behind their camels."

"That's not a pretty picture—camels with trailers," Dino said between laughing and eating his last can of sand-filled chili. "I can't wait until tomorrow morning to move to Malta and some decent food without the sand."

The Battle Over Egypt Intensifies

The battle between Italian and British forces had spilled over the Egyptian border from Libya, but the Italian attack had stalled because of long supply lines. The roads leading from Central Egypt to Alexandria were safe from the battle 300 miles west, but British traffic moving to the battle line would not be safe.

The Alexandria airport was busy with British troops, civilians, and businesspeople trying to either leave the country or conducting business. Mass confusion best described the airport. Seems weird that so many Italian civilians and businesspeople still operated in the area while their armies were trying to take Egypt.

Alsos Headquarters had directed the duo to go to a luggage locker to pick up their Italian journalists' papers, cash, clothing, and cameras needed to complete their disguise.

As Dino approached the luggage locker, John remained seated watching for anyone showing interest in the two men dressed as Bedouins. No one seemed interested as Dino took the contents of the locker and motioned for John to follow him into the restroom. "Change into these." John told Dino as he passed him the clothing for the trip to Malta.

"What are we going to do with the *tobs* and kufiyah?" Dino asked while changing from the Bedouin clothing and into the civilian clothing more suitable for an Italian journalist and his photographer assistant.

"We are to place them in the luggage and return them to the locker for future OSS use," John replied as the two men changed clothing.

The Italian airliner sat ready for boarding for the estimated five-hour flight to Malta. Security was non-existent. Passengers fighting for position in one line or another to either leave the airport or board a plane. There were British soldiers watching the crowds but not really interested in stopping anyone.

Team 2 in Malta

In late 1942, the Germans bombed Malta constantly and had begun a siege of the island that failed. Unfortunately, there was damage everywhere. The German High Command ordered the bombing and siege in retaliation for the damage done to Axis shipping. The islands held a controlling and vital location in the middle of the Mediterranean and kept much of the needed Axis supplies from reaching North Africa. The island had been damaged but not destroyed. Axis supply ships were drastically needed in the North African campaign to continue the war against the British in Egypt. German and Italian forces needed the supplies to continue their attack on Egypt to control air traffic out of Alexandria and oil supplies through the Suez Canal. Malta was a thorn in the sides of German High Command.

Malta was the major reason why the Italian and German forces were turned away from the Egyptian border.

Flight to Malta

The navigator of the Italian aircraft met John and Dino at the ladder leading to the interior of the plane and their assigned seats. "Take your seats, gentlemen. It's a five-hour flight to Malta, if the weather holds. This time of year, sandstorms can form in minutes and force an aircraft out of the air," the navigator continued. "Surprised to find another OSS agent on board?"

"Yes, and glad to meet you," John said. "I know what you mean about the dust," John said. "We were in several. The fine sand was everywhere, even in our canned rations."

"Your contact in Malta will be an OSS officer named Murphy." The navigator said as he closed the door and moved toward the cockpit.

Six hours later, the Italian airliner landed hard, bounced twice, before settling onto the hard dirt track. Just missing many of the German bomb craters. "Good luck, gentlemen." The navigator said as he opened the passenger door to help the two men out of the aircraft.

"Where are we, and where is Murphy?" John asked as he climbed down the ladder to the ground.

"Might as well still be in the Alexandria from the looks of this place," Dino voiced his displeasure again to the move. "Maybe that's him coming in the lorry." Dino added while watching the approaching truck.

"Welcome to RAF Hal Far airport. Hope your trip was comfortable," Murphy said, knowing how uncomfortable the flight had become during the war. "My name is Major Murphy Donnelly, your tour guide while in Malta." Murphy said while shaking the hands of John and Dino.

Both men marveled at the beautiful creature shaking their hands. Even in baggy civilian clothing and cap, she showed striking beauty. Her blond hair and bright smile changed the general attitude of the two men. She was not what they expected.

John finally took a breath and regained his senses. "Glad to meet you, Major. I thought we were meeting the typical OSS male spook with thick glasses."

"I hope you aren't too disappointed," Murphy said while helping load their belongings into the lorry.

"Oh, I'm not disappointed. Just embarrassed. You are a pleasant surprise. Colonel Powers should have told us about you."

"He probably didn't think about it. When he and I met, we were dodging prying eyes. I disguised myself as a delivery person with black hair during our last meeting."

Dino was still uncomfortable from the long flight and felt neglected and left out of the conversation between John and Murphy. "Where will we be staying tonight?"

"You won't be staying here. Your Italian contact is to meet you at a café in St. George's on the east coast. You probably won't see me again." Murphy explained.

John interrupted. "I'm sorry to hear that. I would like to have bought you a drink to thank you for taking us to the rendezvous."

"It's not too late to buy me a drink." Murphy said while displaying those gorgeous hazel eyes and bright smile. "You will meet your Italian contact at 2100 hours at the sidewalk café close to the port. It should be warm but not hot with the breeze coming off the Mediterranean, should be comfortable."

"Looking forward to it." John added.

Dino felt excluded from their conversation again and entertained himself by watching the traffic as they moved away from the airport. "Did you notice the gray Citron following us?" He asked. "It has been on our tail since we left the airport."

"No, speed up Murphy. Make two right turns to see if they continue to follow us." John directed.

Murphy nursed the old lorry around two right turns, fighting the steering wheel for control. She began watching the rearview mirror while trying to figure who could be following them. Speed was the main issue. The Citron could overtake the larger and heavier lorry, no matter how hard they tried to evade them. The advantage the lorry had was its weight and bumper height above the ground. If the Citron should try to force them off the road or stop in front of them, the Citron would be squashed like a bug.

"The Citron is following us," Murphy announced. "Can't make this thing move any faster?"

"I have an idea." Dino said while searching for something in his bag. "Don't do anything until I'm ready. Slow down and move into the middle of the road. That will force him to drive close to the side of the road when he pulls up next to us. That Citron rides low on the road. When he pulls up next to us, I will tell you when to turn into him."

"Here he comes. What are you going to do?" Murphy asked while still fighting with the old lorry's steering wheel.

"Now turn into him." Dino said while pointing his Graflex press camera toward the driver of the Citron. The flashbulb temporally blinded the driver, and he failed to see the high curb and drainage ditch. The driver slammed on his brakes, but it was too late. The Citron hit the curb and continued into the ditch. The sound of metal on concrete and broken headlights suddenly pointing in different directions proved to be the end of the chase.

"Should we stop to check on them?" John asked. He knew the answer before he finished his question.

Chapter 19

TEAM 1 MOVES TO MOROCCO

Martinez picked the route from the lava fields in Libya leading to El Guettar, Tunisia. It was ideal for moving fast without attracting attention. The quicker, the better for the team moving to Morocco. Allied troops occupied the valley outside the El Guettar pass, making the trip further west toward Morocco appear safe.

Fortunately for the team, an American colonel stopped the team as they passed over the hill leading into the valley. "Halt!" the colonel's aide ordered. "Who are you, and what are you doing here?" Several heavily-armed American soldiers stood by his side to enforce the order.

"Blake Runnels, Alsos team 1, heading to Morocco, sir." Blake answered while trying to appear calm.

"What is the mission of your team?" the colonel ordered.

"We're with OSS and British MI6 recording battles and communicating results to headquarters. We have been working out of a lava field in Libya until ordered to Morocco." Blake answered, still trying to stop the shaking.

"Is your team responsible for those camel dung mines?" The colonel asked.

"Yes, sir. It wasn't our idea though. Their purpose was to stop tanks, but the supply trucks ran over them before the tanks arrived."

"Great!" The colonel responded. "Your reputation proceeds you. You will place more of them on the slopes of this hill," the colonel continued. "The Germans have recently changed their tactics by using motorized half-tracks and motorcycle sidecars to help advancing troops while their 88mm guns provide cover. Rommel has moved to Mainland Italy and left General Von Arnim in charge of the Axis forces, including fifty tanks positioned in the pass, and expected to attack soon. I need you to help defend our artillery positioned just over this hill."

"I can't wait to see how effective camel dung is in battle." The colonel said.

"I'm sorry, sir, our orders call for us to proceed to Morocco." Blake said.

"Your orders have changed soldier. You and your team will help defend this high ground. Headquarters told me to move my headquarters off this hill and retreat. I will, like hell!" The colonel explained. "Anyone who pulls out will be shot by me personally for desertion. That includes you and your team."

"Do you have any questions?"

"No sir. What do you want us to do?" Blake stop shaking long enough to agree to help.

"That's more like it, soldier. Take your team and plant your mines on the slope leading to the artillery pieces just beyond the top of that hill. Disguise the mines with the dung and get out of the mine filed quickly. The German attack is eminent. The advancing troops might dodge the mines, but the half-tracks and motorcycle sidecars won't have time."

"Sir, we sighted several Jock columns east of here that could harass the German forces if you can find them." Nate volunteered. "They were moving south into the desert when we saw them yesterday about 10 miles east of here."

"Thanks, soldier." The colonel said as he climbed into the waiting jeep to take him to his headquarters bunker. "Get those mines planted and move back behind the artillery pieces. Report to

Captain Flowers for further orders. Give the sighting information of those Jock columns to the captain. We can use General Hobart's 7th Armored Division to harass the Germans when they attack. Call them Jock columns or Desert Rats, I don't care. I can't wait to see them in action."

Sergeant Martinez helped Nate place the mines along the slope as directed by the colonel. "Who is that colonel?" Martinez asked while carefully placing the mines about 12 feet apart. "I guess we should be glad he stopped us. We could have wandered into that pass full of Germans looking for a fight."

Blake was moving the mines from their lorry when Captain Flowers approached. "Let me help you with those," Flowers said while passing a container of mines to Nate and Martinez.

"Thank you, Captain," Blake said while unloading another container.

"You guys are lucky the colonel spotted you before you wandered into that canyon. You would be pushing up daisies by now. The colonel told me to help you with the mines and get some food and shelter for tonight, if we're still alive."

"Thanks again, Captain. The colonel is very persuasive, and yes, we would appreciate some fresh rations and a place out of the sand tonight." Blake said. "The colonel told us to give you the sightings of several Jock columns we passed yesterday. He wants to use the Desert Rats to defend this hill. This is Nate Simmons and Sergeant Martinez. I am Blake Runnels. We are team 1 of the Alsos mission." Blake said while unloading another container of mines and covers.

"Welcome to Hill 643," Flowers said. "Our position above the valley has kept the Germans from advancing into the valley and the desert beyond. Our artillery has helped avoid a frontal attack, but we expect the Germans to mount an attack anytime. They have fifty half-tracks and motorcycle sidecars and a large force of troops just waiting to attack."

"What is the colonel's name? I would like to send him a thank-you note." Nate asked sarcastically as Flowers continued to describe the battle plan.

"His name is Col. Jack Hawkins of Tulsa, Oklahoma, Black-Jack for short." Flowers answered.

Nate was embarrassed by his remark about the colonel but decided to continue his complaining. "We are a support team and not to be involved in enemy battles. We are to watch and report our findings to headquarters in London. Blake and I are journalists, while Martinez is a retired army sergeant." Nate continued. "Why Black-Jack? The colonel isn't black."

"No, the colonel isn't black, but everything else is." Flowers volunteered. "Black boots, black hand grips on his pistol, black braces or suspenders—everything he can wear is black." Flowers went on. "Me too, I am a communications specialist caught on this hill while trying to improve communication between the colonel and headquarters."

"I guess this war is inconvenient for everyone." Blake finally said. "We are to report to British headquarters in Morocco by tomorrow night."

Chapter 20

THE SIDEWALK CAFÉ

"What time is it?" Dino asked for the third time in the last thirty minutes.

"Relax, it's time you stop asking. Enjoy your drink, it's probably the first drink you have had that didn't include desert sand since you arrived in Libya. The Italian underground contact will find us anytime now," Murphy said, still trying to decide why the Citron was following them. "Did you recognize those guys following us?" Murphy asked.

"No, the dark windows obscured their faces and the number of occupants." John answered while sipping on the great native drink that he could not pronounce. "They didn't have the right equipment if they were trying to stop us. That low-slung Citron couldn't push a lorry off the road. Where are you heading from here?" John asked Murphy while still trying to decide whether he liked her or just appreciated her help. She was beautiful and smart, but she was an OSS agent. Most spooks appear far from the gentile. Her hazel eyes kept flashing in his mind, causing him to question his interest, while he was wishing he could spend more time with her.

"I am to stay here until the Allied forces clear the Axis from Sicily before joining another OSS team heading into Mainland Italy," Murphy stated while trying to decide if John was being nosy or really interested. "We may cross paths again in Southern Italy. Let's try to stay in touch."

"How can I contact you?" John asked.

"Colonel Powers has my contact information. It's an encrypted radio message center found next door to your headquarters in London. You can leave me a message there, assuming Powers will allow you to use the service."

"Do we have time for something to eat?" Dino asked while tiring of asking for the time. "I would love a piece of chicken or a burger."

"Burgers are hard to find in Malta, but with more arriving American troops preparing for Operation Torch, there will be more requests for them. *Bigilla* is my favorite. It is a thick paste of broad beans with garlic." Murphy explained. "Another favorite is *Hobz*, which is a round of bread dipped in olive oil, rubbed with tomato sauce, and filled with a mixture of tuna, onion, garlic, tomatoes, and capers."

"That sounds good, but what about something sweet?" Dino asked.

"You can usually find cannoli and *Helwa tat-Tork*, which is a sweet sugary mixture of crushed and whole almonds," Murphy said while checking her watch again for the Italian underground. "They are late."

"Do you have your radio that we could contact our headquarters?" John asked. "We haven't checked in since last week, and we are late in providing information on our progress toward Sicily."

"Sure, it's under the passenger seat. Be quick, we must still be careful where Italian or German Intelligence could intercept our messages," Murphy continued. "They still have spies in the area to locate and destroy radios."

"Glacier, this is Eyeball. Over," John keyed the radio and waited for the response from headquarters. After a short pause and several seconds of static, the radio responded. "Eyeball, this is Glacier. Over. Do you read me?" John responded in the affirmative to the radio operator.

"Loud and clear, Eyeball." came the response.

"We are at point 2 and awaiting contact before moving to point 3. Over." John pointed out to headquarters that they were in Malta awaiting the Italian underground to move to Sicily.

"Roger, Eyeball. Papa has a message for you when you arrive home." The static returned to the radio as headquarters signed off. John followed by shutting down his radio and replacing it under the seat of the lorry.

"Papa has a message for us when we reach Sicily," John told Dino and Murphy. "Colonel Powers uses Papa when he has important information or mad about something. Whatever it is, it will have to wait until we reach Sicily."

The waiting for their Italian contact was becoming painful. The three sat at their table without speaking for a few minutes. There was nothing more to say, and the contact was forty-five minutes late.

Out of frustration, Murphy ordered another round of drinks. A few minutes later, the waiter reappeared bearing a bottle of Italian Lambrusco wine. "Wait a minute," Murphy said. "We didn't order wine." The waiter did not stop to correct his mistake and disappeared behind the bar.

As Murphy examined the bottle, she noticed a small piece of paper attached to the label. She opened the note, read it, and quickly crammed the crumpled note into her pocket. Without saying a word, she stood and motioned to John and Dino to follow. The party moved beyond the bar and pushed through a brightly-beaded curtain to find the waiter pointing toward an old Renault parked by the back door. Murphy recognized the old car and driver immediately as another OSS agent and his favorite getaway car.

"Hello, Murphy. How are you? Tired of waiting?"

"No, we were about to uncork a great bottle of Lambrusco. And yes, I am fine." Murphy said while slipping five American dollars into the waiter's hand in recognition for his help. "Why are you here?" Murphy asked thinking the Italian underground was to contact them.

"Your plans have changed. Your Italian contact noticed a dark Fiat parked two doors down the street. They suspected it was German Intelligence and alerted us to move the meeting point. They will meet you on the eastern shore at the port city of Marsaxlokk, where they're prepared to leave immediately."

"That will work," Murphy said. "However, you haven't answered my question—why are you here instead of your regular post on Gozo Island?"

"My orders were to follow a lorry from the airport with two OSS agents on board to this sidewalk café as a security measure. Unfortunately, the lorry forced my beautiful Citron off the road over a curb and into a ditch. I found the lorry after changing vehicles. I should have known you were driving the lorry that forced me off the road."

"Were you assigned to protect us?" Dino asked.

"Yes, but a flash of bright light caused me to lose control of the car. All I could see was the lorry moving into my lane. I tried to stop, but you crowded me off the road."

"I'm sorry," Dino said. "That was my idea. I used the flash from my press camera, not thinking you were coming to help us. I thought you were German Intelligence trying to stop us."

"I wish headquarters would tell us when we're followed for our protection," Murphy said surprised by the lack of communication between agents and headquarters. "Get moving. I'll see you later," Murphy said as the Renault moved away from the café.

The waiter had not cleared the table as Murphy returned. She took a seat and invited the waiter to join her for a glass of fine wine. Murphy and the waiter seated at the table should reassure the Fiat. The agents were still waiting for their Italian contact.

Unfortunately, the dark Fiat parked at the curb began to move. It passed the café slowly then sped away toward the waterfront.

"I need to use your telephone," Murphy said. "I must alert headquarters. The Fiat is following them. "Do you think the Fiat contains German Intelligence?"

"The telephone is under the bar to your left. Yes, probably German Intelligence," the waiter responded.

Murphy was frantic. She had alerted OSS Headquarters about

the moving Fiat and completed her call but still felt she needed to do more to protect the three agents headed to the waterfront. The only available transport was the old lorry. It wasn't fast, but it was dependable and could possibly stop the Fiat before reaching the waterfront.

Chapter 21

THE BATTLE BEGINS

The sound of German heavy equipment filled the air.

"Artillery will precede the tank attack," Captain Flowers explained to the Alsos team crouched in a corner of the headquarters bunker. "The Germans have changed their tactics recently by using motorcycles with sidecars and mounted machine guns to support ground troops, allowing the artillery to fire from stationary positions and more accurate shelling. We will attack their artillery before they can complete their set-up procedure," Flowers said.

"Won't that make their artillery sitting ducks for our artillery?" Nate asked.

"Yes, they will be more vulnerable, but our artillery is less accurate and effective because we remain mobile," Flowers said. "We will direct our first artillery volleys at the German artillery before moving to a more defensible position and change the target to the advancing half-tracks and troops. The plan is to take the enemy artillery out of the battle early or at least most of it."

"Where will the artillery move to concentrate on the half-tracks?" Martinez asked. "I hope they are fast, the first wave of German half-tracks has left the safety of the canyon and heading this way."

"The artillery will move to our right flank and out of sight of the approaching enemy," Flowers continued. "We have spotters at three positions on the slope of the hill to communicate coordinates of the advancing half-tracks and motorcycles. Our Sherman tanks will begin responding to enemy half-track fire as they draw closer."

The colonel was frantically moving pieces around a large map of the hill while keeping an ear open to the various radios from the spotters. "Tell me when the enemy artillery begins to set up . . . Hit them with our artillery before they set up their positions."

"That will expose our artillery positions," a lieutenant said.

"Yes, it will," the colonel responded. "But we will move the artillery quickly to our right flank after several volleys. Any return fire will fall on a deserted position."

"Enemy artillery has moved to their positions and are beginning preparations to fire!" one of the spotters shouted over the radio.

Behind the colonel, a sergeant wearing headphones responded to the radio, "Begin firing."

The earth shook around the bunker from the simultaneous firing of five mobile Howitzer artillery pieces. The firing continued for five minutes followed by silence, while the artillery pieces moved to their new position on the right flank.

Several half-tracks stopped at 9,000 yards, took aim, and fired at the now-deserted Howitzer position.

"Seven of the ten enemy artillery pieces destroyed," the spotter at position 2 reported. "Enemy motorcycles moving to the foothills followed by many foot soldiers at sector 130 at 10,000 yards. They are using the new Zundapp 750cc motorcycle with sidecar with mounted machine gun. There are three soldiers on the motorcycles. I count fifteen Zundapps crisscrossing the battlefield to avoid our tank and artillery fire."

"Order the tanks to fire on the half-tracks," the colonel ordered. From their higher elevation, the Sherman tanks began to pour a barrage of 30mm shells on the approaching half-tracks and continued for ten minutes, forcing them to stop to return fire.

"Colonel, our artillery pieces have successfully moved to our right flank. The 75mm Pack Howitzers are ready to engage the enemy. The new tank destroyers are ready on our left flank, awaiting your orders," the sergeant reported.

"Hawkeye. This is Pigeon One, over." Without waiting for a response, the forward observer continued. "The last of the German artillery has moved to a new position at sector 128 and 12,000 yards. They are beginning to set up."

"Begin firing," the sergeant ordered from behind the colonel as the Howitzers opened fire on the remaining enemy artillery.

"Sir, the spotter from position 3 has provided the sector and yardage for the motorcycles and troops at the base of the hill!" the radio operator shouted.

"Hold your fire on the motorcycles and troops. Order the artillery to continue firing on the enemy artillery. The troops and motorcycles will be in range of our mortar and machine-gun fire at sectors 135 through 140," the colonel ordered.

"Order the spotter at position 3 to retreat. His position will be captured any minute," the colonel ordered.

The noise in the headquarters bunker was deafening. The screams from enemy shelling still aimed at the abandoned artillery position and Sherman tanks were excruciatingly painful. Alsos team 1 remained huddled in the corner safely out of the battle and amazed at the noise and activity.

"I wonder if the colonel was able to contact the Jock columns," Blake asked Major Flowers. "Their services would be handy now."

"They must travel 25 miles before they arrive," Major Flowers said. "Probably too late for this battle. The 'Desert Rats' were formed by British Colonel Jock just for this kind of battle." Captain Flowers went on. "Several of the half-tracks are approaching the camel dung minefield. We will know soon if they work."

"Hold your fire," the sergeant ordered the Howitzers to cease firing. "Sir, we destroyed the enemy artillery."

"Order the Howitzers to begin firing on the half-tracks and troops," the colonel ordered.

"Fire when ready," the sergeant ordered as the Howitzers directed their fire on the half-tracks.

The half-tracks were firing on the Sherman tanks and the new position of the artillery on the right flank. An explosion rocked the right flank. "Sir, two of the Howitzers were hit and the ammunition store destroyed."

"Captain Flowers get out there with more shells!" The colonel ordered. "Use the Alsos team to help move the shells and tend to the injured."

"Yes, sir." Flowers said as he motioned for the Alsos team to follow him.

"Sergeant get ready for the wounded from the artillery position," the colonel ordered.

"Yes, sir." The sergeant said while ordering two medics to standby their radios. "Expect some bad ones, the ammunition store exploded."

"Get those tank destroyers ready!" The colonel ordered.

"Awaiting your orders, Colonel." The sergeant answered.

"Begin firing!" The colonel ordered. "Take some of the pressure off the artillery while they regroup."

"Sir, several half-tracks destroyed or disabled." The sergeant said. The overmatched Shermans performed well from the high ground. The motorcycles were in range as the mortars and machine-gun placements opened fire on them.

Suddenly, one of the half-tracks hit a land mine and burst into flames. The crew could not evacuate before the flames ignited the munitions and exploded.

Another of the half-tracks hit a land mine but only lost one of its tracks. It isn't moving, making it an easy target for the Howitzers. Within seconds, it burst into flames.

The fire on the enemy half-tracks discouraged the motorcycles and foot soldiers. They began to take cover as artillery and tank fire continued to rain down on them.

"Sir, the tank destroyers have slowed the advance of the half-tracks and troops." The sergeant reported. "They are beginning to retreat."

"We have them on the run!" The colonel shouted. "Continue firing until they are out of range. The heavy armor of the new tank destroyers and their armor-piercing shells have stopped the half-tracks, and the camel dung minefield really helped."

Smoke, dust, and the smell of cordite were everywhere. Some small arms fire persisted, while the shelling from the half-tracks ceased. The distant cry for medics could be heard from the wounded enemy soldiers on the slopes of the hill.

"Move our wounded to the mobile hospital," the sergeant ordered as the German retreat continued.

"Sir, the Jock columns have arrived!" The radio operator shouted. "What are your orders?"

"Let me speak to the commander." The colonel said while heading for the radio. "They can help dispose of the motorcycle-mounted soldiers and machine guns."

The colonel said over the radio. "This is Col. Jack Hawkins. Who am I speaking to?" There was a pause before the sergeant of the Jock column squad answered.

"Sgt. James Brighton, sir." The leader said. "We are at your disposal, sir. What are your orders?"

"Hello, Sergeant, just in time for the party." The colonel said. "Glad you could join us, although you are a little late. Are you the Desert Rats?"

"Yes, sir, and I guess we have earned the title, but no one wants to call us a Jock column." Sergeant Brighton answered. "We try to attack fast quietly and retreat just as quickly."

"Your squad could do us a favor, if your British commander will allow." The colonel said. "The Germans have started using motorcycles with sidecar-mounted machine guns and very effectively. Could you chase them down the hill and destroy them?"

"With pleasure, sir." Brighton said. "My boss might be upset, but he will get over it. Where will we find those motorcycles?"

"They are providing cover for the retreating foot soldiers behind the German half-tracks. They should be about 12,000 yards from our position, heading into the canyon. Stay off the slope of the hill where we have set up camel dung minefield."

"I'm not sure what that is, but we will avoid it." The sergeant answered. "We will let you know what happens."

"They aren't going home." The colonel announced. "They're waiting for reinforcements. Both Italian and German forces are preparing for a counterattack. Get those dead tanks off the hill, they provide cover for their foot soldiers." Colonel Hawkins ordered.

"Move the tank destroyers and artillery to our flanks to prepare for a flanking movement by the Germans. Get more of those camel dung mines placed closer to the base of the hill." The colonel continued.

"Come on, you guys, you heard the colonel." Blake said as the Alsos team moved to the old lorry, surprisingly undamaged by the battle.

The mines were finally placed as Colonel Hawkins appeared in his jeep. "The camel dung-covered mines destroyed or disabled five of the half-tracks, six of the motorcycles, and an estimated 750 German soldiers," the colonel said. "I hope no one ever hears that one of my best battle plans consisted of camel dung mines."

"My lips are sealed, Colonel." Blake said. "You saved our butts. We were planning to drive our lorry directly into the massed German forces in the canyon. We will be late to our new post in Morocco, but at least we aren't prisoners of war or shot and pushing up daisies." Blake added.

"Yeah, me too," Nate added. "The cannon fire might have damaged my shirt."

Sergeant Martinez was quiet. He had experienced battle before. "I had forgotten how loud and dirty battle is. It continues to remind me of man's inhumanity to man."

"Thank you for your help," the colonel said. "Take the long way around the pass, and you should be safe. Good luck, gentlemen." The colonel saluted the three men standing at attention, jumped into his jeep, and headed back to his bunker.

Chapter 22

Murphy Chasing the Germans

"Come on!" Murphy shouted at the old lorry. "Move faster."

There were several roads leading to the waterfront. The fastest road was the most direct, but Murphy didn't know which road the OSS agents or the dark Fiat had taken.

Murphy pushed the old lorry to its limits. It was speeding along at a breakneck speed of about 30 kilometers per hour. Its noisy engine whined as Murphy fought with the steering wheel to keep it on the road. The right headlight had broken in contact with the Citron, making turning especially dangerous in the late afternoon light.

The 8 kilometers to the waterfront took forever. As the old lorry topped the hill leading to the front gate to the harbor, Murphy sighted the dark Fiat parked beside the road about two blocks from the gate. *What are they doing, and who are they?* Murphy thought. *They must be expecting the Renault and the three OSS agents, but why?*

Murphy shut off the engine and headlights of the old lorry but continued to roll down the gentle slope toward the parked Fiat.

Chapter 23

RESISTANCE FIRES ON THE GERMANS

"What was that?" Nora flinched at the gunfire heard from beyond the gate to the Italian Resistance boat dock. "Start the engine and tell Enzo to join me on deck," she told Roberto.

"Enzo, Nora wants you on deck," Roberto whispered over the intercom. "There is gunfire at the gate."

Enzo quickly joined his sister on deck of the old fishing vessel. He and his sister managed the few remaining members of the Italian resistance in Southern Italy and were using the fishing boat as headquarters. Many captured members of the underground had suddenly disappeared at the hands of the Gestapo.

Nora and Enzo were more familiar with Northern Italy, where they had worked with John and Dino before to recruit two prominent Italian physicists to work with the Manhattan Project. The remaining underground were taking refuge in Southern Italy and posing as fishermen to avoid arrest which required moving constantly. Thus, the fishing boat was perfect for their purposes.

"It sounds like our friends are attracting attention already," Enzo whispered as he joined his sister. "Is the gunfire directed at them?" Roberto joined Enzo armed with a Remington 1911 pistol.

Enzo took his preferred M1A1 Garand .30-caliber rifle, both prized weapons earned by helping recruit the two physicists as they joined the Manhattan Project. "Follow me," Enzo directed Roberto. "We must support the two agents as they enter the gate," The two men approached the gate carefully to find the occupants of an old lorry and Fiat exchanging gunfire. The main road formed a wide Y before entering the gate. "Which vehicle contains our friends?" Enzo whispered while moving closer to the old lorry.

The other OSS agent in the Renault pulled up behind the old lorry where Murphy had parked, watching the Fiat. "Who is shooting at the lorry?"

Murphy stopped firing at the Fiat and moved to the back of the lorry as the other OSS agent joined her. "I don't know for sure, but I suspect they are German secret service looking for Alsos team 1."

Enzo and Roberto approached the two vehicles as they had not been able to identify John and Dino in either vehicle. "Work your way around the brush and trees and come up next to the Fiat." Enzo directed. "I will approach the lorry and Renault from the opposite direction. Let me know what you find on your radio, once you reach the Fiat. Stay low and out of sight. Either side might shoot you. One of these vehicles will contain our friends from America. Unfortunately, I don't know which one," Enzo followed a line of brush to the opposite side of the lorry and Fiat to try to identify the occupants of the vehicles. Enzo keyed his radio and asked. "Can you see the occupants of the Fiat?"

"No, it is too dark," Roberto reported from the other side of the Fiat.

Enzo was close to the lorry and Renault when he overheard voices. At first, he didn't recognize the language but soon recognized it as an English voice. Then he heard the unmistaken voice of John and an unfamiliar female voice speaking a more familiar English.

Enzo finally decided to test the voices but from the safety of his cover in the bushes. "John, is that you?"

"That sounds like Enzo," John said. "Where are you?"

"Don't shoot me," Enzo said. "I'm coming from the bushes to your left."

Enzo quickly joined John and Dino behind the lorry. "It's good to see you," John said while the three men embraced.

"It's good to see you too, but let's get out of here," Enzo said while keying Roberto by the Fiat.

"Hide yourself before firing two shots at the Fiat," Enzo told Roberto. "We will fire a few shots at the same time to scare them away. We will fire when we hear your shots. It will sound like we have surrounded them."

"BANG, BANG!" The clear sound of the Remington .45-caliber weapon broke the silence, followed by a volley of several shots fired from the opposite direction.

The Fiat sped away, still firing shots from the passenger side.

"Enzo, stop shooting, I'm coming out!" Roberto said as the taillights of the Fiat disappeared down the hill. "Let's get out of here, a truck is coming."

"Probably British military police," Murphy said while restarting the lorry to leave the scene. "Stay out of trouble, and perhaps I'll see you again in Sicily," She directed her comments to John and Dino as she drove the old lorry away, followed by the other OSS agent in the Renault.

"Hurry, our boat is just beyond the gate!" Enzo said, ducking back into the brush to avoid the gate. John and Dino were right behind, followed by Roberto.

Just inside the gate the tall brush hid the four men from sight of the truck as it drove through the gate and stopped. Nothing was visible. No cars were shooting at one another. The scene that seconds earlier was a battleground heard from the guard shack was now empty. A grumpy sergeant ordered the truck to turn around and return to the guard shack. Another family feud or perhaps just some teenagers having fun and shooting road signs.

"The boat is just ahead," Enzo told John and Dino. "Do you have everything you will need?"

"Everything to appear as two Italian journalists," Dino answered. "Is Nora with you?"

"Yes, she is expecting you," Enzo said as the four men climbed aboard the boat. "I'll raise the anchor and join you in the galley." John and Dino headed for the galley escorted by Roberto.

The boat began to move slowly away from the small pier. Stealth movement was more important than speed to remain unnoticed by harbor authorities. The boat was moving without its lights as fog began to descend over the cool waters. It was not likely that anyone would notice a fishing boat leaving the port at this hour.

A faint drone of a large diesel engine sounded as the three men moved silently through the ship toward the galley. The smell of decaying fish bait and diesel fuel added to the genuine appearance of the fishing boat.

As the three men entered the door to the galley, the fishing boat odors disappeared and were replaced by the smell of strong Italian coffee and something sweet. Dino missed breakfast and lunch and finally gave way to his urges. "I'm hungry. Is it too late to make a sandwich?"

"Yes, it is too late for a sandwich," Nora said as she stood to greet the two men. "There is plenty of coffee, cannoli, and fresh bread. I see that you haven't changed much from our last meeting, hungry as usual and making more enemies."

"Hello, Nora," Dino said while reaching out to her. "You haven't changed much either, still beautiful and managing the underground. It's good to see you again."

John finally got a chance to embrace Nora as a silence fell between the two old friends. "Thanks for saving our hides again. Those guys in the Fiat were not real friendly."

"Glad we could help," Nora repeated. "We must get underway if we are to make our appointed trip to Sicily."

Nora turned from the two men, wished them good night, and went to the control room to supervise the long trip to the southeastern tip of Sicily. "I'll see you in the morning." She and Roberto left the galley, while Enzo, John, and Dino began to discuss their mission and fill the stomach of poor starving Dino.

"Any idea who those guys were?" Enzo asked while spreading a map of Sicily on the table. "Probably German Intelligence, but why start a firefight in British territory? Risky. They must have known who you were."

"Murphy will tell OSS and Major Powers," John said while tearing off a big chunk of bread with some cheese before handing the bread to Dino and Enzo. "Now that we are away from Malta, there won't be much of a threat from German Intelligence, but there will be German and Italian submarines and patrols to contend with."

Nora was at the controls of the fishing boat skirting the Malta coastline heading east toward the open water of the Mediterranean when the radio interrupted her concentration.

"Glacier. This is Eyeball, over," Said the keyed call to Dino and John from headquarters.

"Eyeball. This is Yard Bird, over." Nora answered.

"Yard Bird. This is Eyeball. Papa is waiting for his two daughters to come home, over."

"Eyeball. This is Yard Bird. On their way home. Over and out." Nora ended the call from headquarters and sent Roberto to tell John and Dino that Powers needed to speak with him.

"Papa is looking for his two daughters." Roberto told Dino with a big grin on his face. "Are you late coming home from a dance with a hairy legged boy?"

Chapter 24

ROAD TO RABAT

"Can't you make this old bucket of bolts move any faster?" Nate asked.

"My foot is on the floorboard now. It won't move any faster," Martinez yelled over the noise of the old truck. "We have three days to make Rabat, and its only 400 miles. Try to relax."

"Let's stop at the next town for the night, I'm beat," Blake reasoned after hearing the banter between Martinez and Nate. "What's the next town?"

"Hassi is next, but it's small. Next is Ouargla, much larger and it has one of the famous souk markets, with endless rows of stalls selling local produce," Nate answered while studying the small information booklet provided by Headquarters. "There will be food and drink, but I don't know about a place to stay. We may have to camp out in the lorry."

"I don't care where we stay, I can sleep on a tile floor. I'm too tired and have saddle-sores from driving all day." Martinez said.

"This booklet is full of important information," Nate said. "Besides the souk, this area is where the desert rose is found?"

"What the heck is a desert rose? I can't believe any flower would grow in this heat." Blake said while wiping the sweat from his brow.

"They are pink sandstone formations shaped like a small rose,"

Martinez said while studying the road map. "They are formed by the shifting sands that collect an occasional raindrop. I can't imagine what force makes them hard and appear as a rose."

"How far to Ouargla?" Blake asked.

"About 50 miles," Martinez answered. "I could sure use a bath and a beer. How about you guys?"

"You could use a shave and a deodorant too." Blake told Martinez jokingly.

"We must wait until we reach Rabat for a bath and change of clothes," Nate said. "No clothes change out here in the desert."

"Take a bath here and wear dirty clothes for the rest of the trip doesn't sound like fun to me." Martinez answered.

"I think Martinez should still try a deodorant just to keep the camels away." Blake said while jabbing Martinez in the ribs, almost causing him to lose control of the lorry.

"You gringos don't smell too good either." Martinez quipped and jabbed Blake in return.

A Bath but Dirty Clothes

The trio did have to spend the night in the lorry but didn't care or couldn't care after all the local alcoholic beverages.

They left early the next day to avoid the hottest part of the day. It was already 90 degrees at 0830 hours and climbing.

The trio ate well and drank anything that was liquid the previous night. They felt eager to reach Rabat. After sleeping in the old lorry, refueling, and refilling all their containers with water, they left the comforts of Ouargla and joined the traffic heading west.

"What is all the traffic coming this way?" Blake asked. "Looks like a division size troop movement heading this way. They are both British and American troops moving fast. Pull off the road," Blake directed. "Let's ask someone where they are going, assuming we can get them to stop."

Martinez spotted a six-by-six truck stopped off the road about

400 yards ahead. "There is a carryall truck probably stalled for some reason, we can ask them."

The old lorry pulled off the road across from the carryall. Fast-moving trucks were heading east. During a short break in the traffic, Martinez sprinted across the road to speak to the driver of the carryall.

"Do you need some help?" Martinez asked.

"No, thanks, help is following this column and should be here in about ten minutes," The driver of the carryall said. "Thanks anyway."

"Where are you heading?" Martinez asked.

"Most of the Germans are retreating toward Tunis, and many of the Italian forces are moving west out of Egypt and Libya. We have them surrounded with British and Australian troops moving west from Egypt, and we are closing in on them from Morocco. Should be a short time before all Axis forces move toward Sicily." The carryall driver explained.

"Thanks, buddy, we're heading for Rabat. Good luck and try not to get shot." Martinez said. "What is that funny sign on your door?"

"Good luck to you too," the carryall driver said. "That sign is 'Kilroy Was Here,' you will probably see it a lot of them on the way to Rabat."

"What does it mean?" Martinez asked.

"Damned if I know. It has been painted on anything that doesn't move." Was heard as Martinez pulled onto the road to Rabat.

Chapter 25

Team 2 to Sicily

The lights of Pozzallo and Modica, Sicily, came into view shortly after 0200 hours as Dino stared into the darkness off the port side of the old fishing boat.

"When will we make land?" Dino asked Enzo, studying the charts of the various small villages along the southwestern coast of Sicily.

"It will be two more hours; we are not heading toward those lights you now see," Enzo said while pointing to a small port city on the charts. "This is where we are heading, well, northwest of those lights. The Germans and Italians are checking all shipping along the coast but have paid little attention to the small fishing villages north of Butera."

As the fishing boat plied the waters along the coast of Sicily, staying 5 miles off the coastline, an Italian patrol boat appeared out of the darkness.

"All stop!" Enzo ordered over the noise of the engine. "Turn off all lights!" He continued.

"What is it?" Nora shouted from below deck. "Are we under attack?"

"No, not yet. Keep your voice down," Enzo ordered. "An Italian patrol boat is approaching with its lights searching the coastline. Fortunately, they are moving fast and searching the coastline. We must not alert them of our presence. No noise or lights until further notice."

"What if we are spotted?" John whispered as he joined Enzo and Dino at the wheel. "Will they board us or ignore us as a local fishing boat?"

"We never know. They have often destroyed an unfamiliar boat in these waters," Enzo explained. "It is best that we remain undetected. If our luck holds, the patrol boat will run with their search lights focused on the coastline, moving fast and pass about 600 yards to our port."

The silence was broken by the sound of a barking dog below deck. "Shut up, Echo!" Nora whispered down the open stairwell leading to the galley. Dino had slipped down into the galley for some coffee and was playing with Echo when he started barking. "Keep him quiet."

"Sorry, I didn't think he would start barking," Dino explained out of embarrassment. "I'll keep him quiet."

Enzo listened intently for any sign that the patrol boat had heard the dog. Several minutes passed before he felt comfortable the patrol boat did not hear the barking and sped past them, heading along the coastline south and away from the fishing boat.

"That was lucky," Enzo whispered to Nora and John. "The patrol boat was leaving the shallow water of the small fishing village of Butera, where we are to contact Luca. Why are the patrol boats now patrolling this area?"

"Do you think the Italians have increased patrols in the area in response to the rumors of a joint operation by British and American forces?" Nora asked John. "Or are they just watching for saboteurs or illicit arms trading?"

"I don't know for sure, but we have been ordered to Sicily and Southern Italy to record something planned soon," John answered. "Dino and I have orders to work with you in the area, but we have not been told what we are to do or why."

"Keep quiet," Enzo ordered as the craft approached the dock. He then sent two flashes of light toward the dock followed by three more after a one-minute pause. There was no response, and he feared the Italian patrol had found their contact or he had gone into hiding. "What could have happened?"

Finally, there were two short flashes of light from the dock. "Get ready to toss a line to Luca," Enzo ordered. "Contact all on board that we have arrived and get ready to leave for the safe house in Riesa quickly to avoid another patrol boat."

Luca tied off the line and came aboard. "Sorry for the delay. I had to dive into the water and hide behind the dock when the patrol boat came by the dock. They almost caught me in the open when they came in with no lights. I thought it was you at first but recognized it finally as an Italian patrol boat and jumped into the water."

"Have the Italians increased patrols in these small villages?" Nora asked. "They almost caught us too. They must suspect something, or they would patrol only the areas south and the larger villages."

"Yes, they started yesterday patrolling this area and south every four hours. They will be back at sunrise," Luca answered. "I have arranged to move your boat further north to another small fishing village after you have unloaded. You must move fast to make the foothills and the safe house before dawn."

Desert What?

"Good of you to let me know where you are," Colonel Powers said sarcastically. "American and British headquarters have been bending my ear about you guys. Seems that trouble follows you around like a little puppy."

"Sorry, sir, we have been busy." Blake answered sheepishly.

"We have answered way too many complaints and requests for your services from both American and British commanders." Colonel Powers said. "Even an Australian commander called embarrassed by the odor of the camel dung covers." Powers continued. "I've had to explain several times that plastic has no odor, and the odor he smells is you guys wandering around without a bath."

Blake chuckled and added. "I know. Then they ask what plastic is . . ." Blake paused before passing the blame for the covers. "It's not my fault, John and Dino asked for them, and you and Lieutenant Townsend had them built."

"I don't apologize for building the damn things," Powers said. "In fact, they have been so successful that I may receive a commendation for them which I will gladly share with you when we next meet," Powers said, suppressing laughter. "A colonel and the Desert Rats have suggested the covers become standard issue in desert warfare. They want to call them desert dung."

"Was that Colonel Hawkins?" Blake asked after several loud giggles. "He actually saved our hides. He kept us from driving into a German encampment preparing for the battle at El Guettar."

Nate, tired of the current silly discussions and interrupted the colonel. "Sir, are we through talking about the dung?" Nate continued. "We were to contact you about a new assignment."

"Nate, you are too sensitive," Powers answered. "But yes, you have a new assignment. It concerns the Straits of Gibraltar, but it's more fun talking about your desert dung."

"What is so important in the straits that it can't wait a couple of days to let us get a bath and a little rest?" Blake asked.

"When you reach Morocco, contact British Intelligence at the embassy in Rabat," Powers directed. "A joint American and British operation involving the Strait of Gibraltar is planned, and your expertise is involved."

"What expertise?" Blake asked. "I'm a journalist."

"Not just you. You, Nate, and Martinez," Powers explained. "Nate is a retired navy special services leader, and Sergeant Martinez knows heavy equipment. We will need you to record the exercise."

"Can you discuss the exercise over the radio?" Blake asked concerned about secrecy.

"No." Powers said. "Your instructions will come from MI6 at the British Embassy."

"Where is team 2?" Blake asked. "Will they be involved with the exercise? If they are, ask them to leave the desert dung in Libya."

After the laughter died down, the static on the radio returned ending the communication.

Chapter 26

OPERATION TORCH

Colonel Powers ordered John and Dino to board a British submarine as it plied the Mediterranean waters south of Butera, Sicily. "You are to proceed to an area in the Atlantic, south of Gibraltar, to monitor and report on the activity of a British Convoy SL 125 as it moves north from Sierra Leone," Colonel Powers paused before mentioning Blakes' request. "Leave the desert dung in Libya."

Colonel Powers continued. "Convoy SL 125 consists mainly of empty cargo ships and a small protective zone of naval vessels moving north destined for Great Britain to reload for another trip to Sierra Leone. You are to report on the progress of Convoy SL 125 as it approaches Morocco and Gibraltar."

Colonel Powers told John and Dino, "Operation Torch has begun and is the preamble to invading mainland Europe. It is a large force of both British and American ships leaving several British ports heading for North Africa by way of the Strait of Gibraltar. SL 125 is headed into the battle zone accidentally," Or so we are told."

Powers reported to John and Dino aboard the British submarine, "The joint flotilla of 1,400 American and British vessels is heading toward Gibraltar destined for the ports cities of Oran, Algiers, and Casa Blanca to bring the battle in North Africa to an end. Prepare to report on Operation Torch progress as it unfolds in the Mediterranean.

American OSS and British SAS agents have reported that a large force of German and Italian submarines have blocked the Strait of Gibraltar, preparing to meet the joint American and British forces as they enter the Mediterranean."

"Wow!" John said. "Sounds like a monstrous battle is about to unfold at the strait. When do you expect the battle to begin?"

"The American and British flotilla is 150 miles north of Gibraltar. It could happen soon," Powers reported. "You are within 60 miles of the reported nine German and twenty-six Italian submarine force that also includes a German squadron of Schellboots patrolling the area of the strait."

"What is a Schellboot?" John asked.

"They are fast and heavily-armed torpedo boats," Powers answered. "Effective in close work with the submarines, they have been responsible for several merchant vessel kills and effective in defending the German submarines caught under fire."

"What is this British Convoy SL 125? Are they part of Operation Torch?"

"I'm not sure," Powers answered. "It may be coincidence that they happen to be leaving Sierra Leone heading north while the flotilla of ships heading for Gibraltar are coming from the north. Whatever the reason, the German and Italian submarines are paying close attention. The mainly-empty merchant ships are heading back to England for more cargo. Information received at Alsos Headquarters suggests the cargo remaining on board one ship is vital to the Allied war effort and part of a shipment of 1,200 tons of U-235 uranium from Belgium Congo all bound for Marseille, France and processing."

"I don't get it." John said. "Why would the British convoy SL 125 be escorting a ship bound for France? It would make more sense for the convoy to continue toward England and an Allied port, especially if the uranium is vital for the Allied war effort."

"You're right," Powers responded. "Doesn't make sense. Unless the shipment of uranium requires processing before it is transported to an Allied port. Whatever the reason, we are ordered to report the progress of SL 125."

"Perhaps, but a processing plant nearby would be in the hands of the Germans, Italians, or Vichy French, and the Allies would lose the shipment." John answered.

"There is a processing plant near Marseille, France, and another at Arles." Powers continued. "Both plants are controlled by Vichy French. The shipment may be destined for those plants, but the Allies would lose the shipment. You are probably right, but we are just following orders."

"Doesn't make sense," John responded. "Unless the Allies are planning to use the ship containing the uranium as bait to entice the Germans to respond to the convoy SL 125, why else would the wolf pack leave their current position controlling the strait and head south toward the approaching SL 125 convoy?"

"Without the German force in the strait, the flotilla of British and American ships can enter the Mediterranean unopposed." Powers explained.

"In that case, the battle planned for the strait will shift to the Atlantic coast south of Morocco. We will be in the thick of the battle, all to control a shipload of U-235 uranium." John responded. "Doesn't sound like a safe place to be. We should be in a prime location to report on the battle."

"I know communications will be interrupted often as your submarine will need to run beyond periscope and radio antenna depths," Powers added. "We will keep our radio open for any transmissions from you and try to stay out of the battle."

"You can count on that, sir." John said and closed the radio transmission.

"Nate, Blake & Martinez in Rabat"

"You're late!" the short British sergeant said as Nate, Blake, and Martinez as the three men reported to the embassy in Rabat as ordered.

"It's their fault." Martinez volunteered while pointing to Nate and Blake.

"You're the slow driver," Nate responded to Martinez' accusation. "All I did was keep you on the right road and out of trouble. Anyway, Blake is the one really at fault because of those damned camel turds."

"I don't care about slow drivers or camel turds or whose fault it is, you have kept your MI6 agent waiting to take you to your next assignment," The British sergeant explained. "And a Colonel Powers has been looking for you too. Now get moving, your transportation is waiting in the basement. Look for a black lorry with a sign reading 'Fresh Fruit and Vegetables' on the side."

"Give us a break," Blake pleaded. "We have been trying to get here for almost a week." Blake answered. "We were kidnapped by a Colonel to fight the battle of El Guettar. Driving 400 miles in the sand and usually in the dark."

"Did Colonel Powers leave a message?" Nate asked.

"No. Now get going. Major Donnelly will be waiting for you."

"I'm sure you were doing your best to be here on time." The sergeant said as he led the embarrassed team out the door and down two flights of stairs to the basement. He found their intended transportation immediately. It was easy. There was just one large black lorry with a fruit and vegetable sign painted on the canvas of the back cover, all other vehicles were white and small sedans.

"There is your contact. Good luck and the next time I see you guys I want to know what the camel dung is all about."

Blake led the team to the waiting lorry jumped on board and turned to acknowledge the driver of the lorry.

"Are you Major Donnelly?" Blake asked as the trio boarded the lorry. "Oh, sorry Major, I guess I should salute."

"Yes. Get on board, we are late," Donnelly said while patiently waiting for the trio of Alsos team members scheduled to board a British cruiser for a classified assignment. She was not happy acting as a taxi driver and having to wait for the three men to arrive.

"Where are you taking us?" Blake asked as he took a seat in the front of the lorry, while Nate and Martinez climbed into the back of the delivery truck.

"You'll see." Donnelly said impatiently while busying herself with driving in the Rabat traffic.

"Are you going to join us?" Blake asked.

"No, I have other assignments." Donnelly answered while busy watching both side mirrors and dodging the heavy traffic.

"Are you being followed?" Blake asked while glancing at the sea of traffic surrounding the lorry.

"Just cautious." Donnelly answered while continuing to check the rearview mirrors.

"Dare I ask about our ride for our next assignment? I was hoping for a shower, some clean clothes, and a steak before we were off again." Blake asked.

"You should have plenty of time for a shower and maybe some clean clothes, but I doubt you will have access to a steak. Should be plenty of beans on the menu though." Donnelly answered with a grin and chuckle.

The lorry left most of the traffic behind as it entered the port facility. "Look for a Higgins boat," Donnelly said. "When you spot it, I will stop long enough for you and your two friends to get out. Don't waste any time, you are already late."

"What's a Higgins boat?" Blake asked. "I have no idea what that is, you will have to point it out to me. I have no experience with naval vessels and would not recognize one from a motorcycle."

"Get ready to jump out of the truck!" Donnelly shouted to Blake and the rest of the team through the curtain between the cab and back of the truck. "I will point out the Higgins boat and stop long enough for you to jump out. It will be your ride to our next assignment."

Blake noted the size of the only boats tied to the pier to . "Those boats won't have a shower or steak. Just barely enough room to keep our feet dry."

Donnelly pointed out the Higgins, stopped a few seconds for

her passengers to jump out, and was preparing to leave when Blake asked a question through the passenger window. "Thanks. Will we see you again?"

"Not likely. Be careful." Donnelly said as the lorry sped away.

Chapter 27

HMS Manchester

"Are you Blake Runnels, Nate Simons, and Sergeant Martinez?" The sailor at the bow of the Higgins asked as the three men approached. "I need to see your orders," The sailor announced. "Get aboard, gentlemen. We are twenty minutes late."

"We don't have any orders," Blake explained as they boarded the Higgins. "This assignment is a big surprise to us, and we have been in the desert for most of the month. Not even close to someplace for orders to be delivered."

"Get aboard. Sit down and brace yourselves for a quick trip."

"Where are we going?" Blake asked as he was thrown backward by the thrust of the suddenly-erupting Higgins engines.

"There, sir," the sailor said while pointing to the moving hulk of the British cruiser, HMS *Manchester*.

"What is that?" Blake asked.

"It is classified as a heavy cruiser, large and heavy but not as large and heavy as some of the battleships," the sailor explained. "The ship is already underway and moving toward the Strait of Gibraltar. I will move alongside before she gains speed to avoid her huge wake," the waves produced by the ship's bulk were growing and could easily swamp the Higgins if not maneuvered correctly.

Blake, Nate, and Martinez were hanging on to the railing of the speeding Higgins, trying to stay calm. "Do you know where the ship is heading?" Blake asked the sailor.

"That's classified, sir." The sailor explained.

"How are we to board that thing?" Martinez asked. "I don't see a stairway or open hatch where we could climb aboard."

Nate had the answer to Martinez's question. "See the rope webbing hanging down the port side of the ship? That is our rope ladder to climb up to the deck."

"Which is the port side? Martinez asked over the roar of the engines.

"We have to climb up the side of the ship on that rope?" Blake and Martinez responded simultaneously.

"Piece of cake." Nate added.

"Maybe for an ex sailor, but us landlubbers would prefer something more stable like an elevator."

The sailor pushed the Higgins to its limits and positioned the hull of the smaller boat between the large wake and the side of the monstrous ship. "You will have only a few seconds to board the cruiser, get ready to take hold of the rope ladders extended from the ships railing. Once you're securely attached to the ladder, I will pull away. Good luck, gentlemen."

Chapter 28

THE SICILY BRIEFING

The small house in Riese was a great meeting place, despite the German and Italian patrols. It was cool, isolated, and smelled of sardines. It was close to the water and a fishermen's retreat for years. The house was vacant several years before Nora offered to rent it for a month. The owner was an old Italian fisherman who had moved to Genoa and welcomed the months' income from rental of the old house. Nora was aware the old man held no loyalty to the Nazis and was assured he would neither question the rental nor compelled to tell the authorities.

The two teams began to arrive at various times and by different means. Sergeants Davis and Martinez arrived early to meet with Nora and Enzo several days before the briefing. They began preparation for the missions and would not take part in the briefing. Colonel Powers had flown into Malta and moved to Riesi by boat with Enzo and the Italian resistance.

The balance of the teams began to arrive just before the briefing.

"Good to see you, Colonel," Nate said. "How was your trip from London? Not much fun traveling during wartime, is it? Can you tell us the details of our new assignment?"

"Good to see you too," Powers answered. "Wait for the briefing."

"How did you get here?" Nate asked Colonel Powers. "I flew into

Malta where I joined Enzo and Nora on their good ship. John and Dino arrived by submarine."

"Never mind, we need to get the briefing started," Powers answered curtly while passing out file folders concerning the proposed mission.

"A little testy today," Nate whispered to Blake while reviewing the file folder.

"He's not pleased about something," Blake whispered in response.

"Let's begin," Powers said firmly. "Sergeants Davis and Martinez arrived earlier and are preparing for their assignments, and you will join them after the briefing," Powers explained. "The French resistance will help team 1 in French territories, while the Italian resistance will help team 2 in Italy. There may be times when it will be necessary to work together. Team 1 will leave here at 2100 hours with Sergeant Martinez and several members of the French resistance. You may remember Adnet as your contact in the Bordeaux region. If I recall, Blake and Martinez enjoyed the work with Adnet and especially his wonderful wines."

Powers continued. "Team 2 will leave an hour later with the Italian resistance. Enzo and Nora will be your escorts again. Try to keep Echo quiet during your mission," The comment directed at Dino.

"My favorite watchdog," Dino said. "Finally found someone around here that loves me."

"What will you be doing?" Blake asked the colonel. "Are you heading back to London?"

"Not likely," Powers answered. "Management of military operations has shifted south with Operation Torch. Probably move our headquarters closer to the action, probably Casa Blanca or Malta."

"If you decide to move to Malta, tell Murphy hello for me," John said. "She kept us out of trouble and helped arrange for Enzo to take us off the island. In fact, she owes me a drink or two."

"The folders and operation plan you received are classified top secret," Powers continued. "You have until 1800 hours to learn and memorize their contents. No copies of the files will be allowed. Nothing can leave this room."

The reaction to the folders grew from disbelief to shock as each team member read their tasks and responsibilities.

Dino's first impression of the briefing announcement was confirmed—the mission was important. It was secret and included Allied forces of several countries. Operation Torch had succeeded in providing a foothold in the Mediterranean, and this new mission was an expansion into other Axis-occupied areas.

Powers continued, "Do not discuss your assignments. Read your folder and, without discussion, return the folders to be destroyed when you feel you have memorized your part in the mission. Secrecy is important, and we don't want to take any chances that we might be overheard. Your assignments match the first phase of the mission, while later phases will change as the Axis forces respond. Do not discuss the details with the resistance. You can discuss your destination and how to get there. However, one of the resistance members passed information to the Axis forces, costing Allied and resistance lives. We don't want that to happen again."

Powers continued. "Report any significant movements to Alsos Headquarters. Use your new code names in your folders and change them often. That concludes the briefing. Good luck, gentlemen. Keep your nose into the wind and your powder dry."

Blake and Nate finished memorizing the file contents before the rest of the teams, excused themselves, and stepped into another room to take a break. Nate had a confused look on his face and finally asked Blake the question bothering him. "What did Powers mean by the phrase, 'keep your nose into the wind and your powder dry'?"

"I think he combined two phrases that I have heard. One sounds like the statement Oliver Cornwell made to his troops crossing a river during a campaign in Ireland in 1856, 'Keep your powder dry.' Wet powder would not burn, and their muskets would misfire. The other part of the phrase sounds more like an early American settler's phrase while traveling in Indian Territory," Blake explained. "The Indians could hear you for 5 miles and smell you for three. I think the phrase was 'Keep your nose in the wind and your eyes along the skyline.' It implied that you should be alert to danger."

"I think Powers intended to stress his previous statement. Good luck, gentlemen, but be careful." Nate answered.

Chapter 29

NEW ORDERS FOR THE MANCHESTER

"I am on my way to the radio room to receive a message from Alsos Headquarters. Come and join me." Morrison told the three card players.

"No, thanks," Blake said between swallows of soda water and belches. "Just tell me where we are going next, and I hope it's on solid ground."

"We're having too much fun taking Blake's matches and enjoying his misery," Nate answered for himself and Martinez. "Hurry back with the messages."

A few minutes later, Morrison returned with the message from Alsos Headquarters. "You got your wish." Morrison said. "The *Manchester* is to shadow the wolf pack heading south toward a merchant fleet. You will be dropped off at some point near Sicily to continue work with the Italian and French resistance."

"What are we supposed to do in Sicily?" Nate asked. "I hope we don't have to place more camel dung mines."

"Details of your assignment are not in the message," Morrison said. "It sounds like the Allies plan to invade Mainland Italy and need you guys to provide a little intelligence. Sounds like fun."

"The push by the Allies into the Mediterranean should end the German presence in North Africa and possibly convince the Vichy French and Italians to join the Allies to beat the Nazis out of Italy and France." Nate guessed.

"Is there more information about the strike force?" Blake asked.

"A portion of the strike force landed on the west coast of Morocco, while the balance of the strike force took positions off the coast of Oran and Algiers. British forces are advancing westward from Egypt," Morrison announced. "It looks like the Allied forces are closing on Tripoli, where thousands of Italian and German troops will be stranded without support from Mainland Italy or supply ships from the Mediterranean."

"More moving, waiting, and nothing to write about is getting old," Nate said. "Maybe once we're back on a hard surface, we will see some action."

"This has been enough action for me." Blake said, still nursing his headache and sour stomach."

"I wonder where John and Dino are and if we will be working with team 2 as the Allies begin to move to Mainland Italy?" Martinez asked. "Probably somewhere enjoying the down time, just like us."

"Anybody know where the mail room is?" Blake asked. "I haven't heard from my lovely wife since we left London."

"Yeah, I'll take you there," Martinez answered. "I'm expecting something from home too."

An hour later, the two men returned to find Nate dozing to the rhythmic movement of the *Manchester*, snoring and sleeping like a baby.

"I'm glad someone can be comfortable in this hunk of British iron," Blake said while watching Nate nap and threatening to awaken him to hear the news from Socorro and Magdalena in Vivian's letter.

"I'll let him read it later," Blake said while opening the letter. "It took three weeks for the letter to reach me," Blake said. "Did you have the same experience?" he asked Martinez.

"I still have not heard from my wife since I left El Paso," Martinez said. "She doesn't write much anyway."

Lieutenant Commander Morrison came by the team's quarters to deliver some news. "We are to drop you guys off at 2200 hours just before leaving the Mediterranean to shadow the wolf pack heading south. We expect a major battle between the wolf pack and the large fleet of mainly-empty merchant vessels. We expect heavy losses of the merchant fleet SL 125, and you will miss the action. The *Manchester* will be able to help protect many of the empty ships heading to England."

Nate jumped as Morrison delivered the news. "Back to work and Morrison interrupted my nap," Nate said. "What have you guys been doing?"

"Vivian sent me a letter three weeks ago and said hi. She has become the Socorro County sheriff, and she said Brandon said hi," Blake explained. "I wonder what I should tell her what we are doing."

"Tell her one of your usual lies, you can't tell her anything else," Nate answered. "You were good at that before you left Socorro."

"The only lie I told her was that you were tall, handsome, and a good angler." Blake added.

"What part of that is a lie?" Nate asked.

"All of it, you dipstick," Blake added. "As the county sheriff, she could arrest you for lying."

"Why would anyone arrest me?" Nate asked. "I have never done anything wrong. As a matter of fact, I never—I stress never—and I never will."

"Wow, who are you?" Blake asked. "The Nate I remember was always in trouble. You must be an impostor or Nate's twin brother that I haven't met."

"Enough of that," Nate finally tired of the criticism. "I wonder what our next assignment will be—where will we go, and who will we work with? It doesn't matter as long as I don't have to place more land mines with camel dung covers."

"Be careful what you ask for, we may be spraying the local grasses with poison sumac." Martinez added.

"Not that stuff!" Nate exclaimed. "It's nasty. I know the exposed soldiers lose their lust for battle because of the scratching and itching, but it doesn't seem fair. I know that it may save their lives by avoiding the fight. Some of the gasses used in the First World War forced the combatants to lay down their weapons but caused loss of sight or injured them in other ways."

"Sumac is a native plant to many of the areas around the Mediterranean, where many of the soldiers would be exposed accidentally. We would just add more sumac to grasses not normally containing the toxin," Martinez added. "It is better than having your body parts removed by a bullet or a mortar shell. At least they recover after a time."

Back at Headquarters: Powers is Concerned

Colonel Powers sat down hard at his desk, still clutching the message just received from John and Dino aboard the British submarine *Endeavor*. It was the first report from the two journalists aboard the submarine, watching the progress of Operation Torch, the massive operation which included 1,400 British and American vessels heading for the Strait to gain passage to the Mediterranean—there was little progress to note. The message was disturbing in that a combined force of German and Italian submarines were forming a blockade of the strait. Clearly, the combined force was ordered there by German High Command in response to reports of the massive strike force heading for the Mediterranean.

John and Dino, aboard the British submarine *Endeavor*, were intently listening to discussions between the captain and his executive officer. "Sonar and radio reports suggest the blockade is complete and the wolf pack patiently waiting for the approaching British and American strike force now some 150 miles from the strait," the executive officer noted.

"We have been ordered to stay out of the conflict, which is imminent," the captain said. "Should be interesting. A large force of cruisers and battleships with air protection involved with a force of submarines confined to a relatively small area of the strait . . ." The captain paused then continued. "Almost sure suicide."

"Sonar reports movement among the submarines," the executive officer said. "Several of the wolf pack are moving toward the strait. Should I contact the strike force to alert them of the movement?"

"Yes, stay in contact with sonar for further movements," the captain ordered. "We will get underway to follow the wolf pack."

"Sir, the radio operator is reporting almost continuous chatter from the German submarines, and sonar reports the entire wolf pack is moving toward the strait," the executive officer said. "We should be able to surface soon as the wolf pack is submerged at 13,000 yards."

John and Dino listened intently to the exchange between the captain and the executive officer as the various maneuvers were performed. The atmosphere in the submarine was tense while the crew carried out the captain's orders. Both John and Dino were unfamiliar with the submarine and marveled at the blind efficiency shown by the crew to their orders. The entire crew was busy doing something seemingly automatic at the slightest mention of an order by the captain.

"I wonder if the German submarines are going to intersect the strike force and almost sure destruction. Or are they planning to leave the strait and head south toward the merchant vessels?" John asked Dino.

"If I were making that decision, I would surely head south." Dino said.

"It only makes sense, but German High Command doesn't always make the decision based on what makes the most sense. Or it could be a diversion to make the Allies think they are heading south for the easier targets and maneuver behind the strike force to attack from the rear," John added. "They could have placed mines in the strait or even use the fast torpedo boats to attack the strike force as they enter the narrows of the strait."

"Alert the strike force that the submarines are moving through the strait and, if they maintain their current heading, will intersect the strike force within four hours," the captain ordered.

"Yes, sir," the executive officer answered as he left the control room heading for the radio room.

"Sir, the radio operator reports that a portion of the strike force has broken formation and heading south toward the west coast of Morocco," the executive officer noted as he returned from the radio room. "Must be part of the strike force plan to invade Morocco."

Minutes later, the radio operator and sonar reported the German submarines had turned south and running parallel to the west coast of Morocco, a move that assured the captain the submarines are planning to attack the merchant fleet heading north from Sierra Leone instead of the strike force. "Alert the strike force of the submarines, move toward the south," the captain ordered. "That leaves the strait unprotected and should allow the strike force uninterrupted passage into the Mediterranean."

"What about the portion of the strike force heading for the west coast of Morocco?" the executive officer asked. "Won't they meet with the submarines running along the coast south?"

"They are separated by 90 miles of open water. The strike force or the submarines should not be in danger of contact if they remain on their current headings and speeds." the captain answered.

"The German submarines have left the battle in the Mediterranean for a few merchant ships," the captain noted. "They must have been ordered to either sink the supply ships or take the vital supplies heading for England. What commander would order his submarines to leave the Mediterranean for a few supply ships, which are reported empty, heading back to England after delivering supplies to Sierra Leone?"

"Prepare to surface," the captain ordered. "We are no longer in danger of being spotted by the departing German submarines. Sonar no longer shows any contacts in the approach to the strait."

"Sir, sonar reports multiple contacts at 10,000 yards heading for the strait!" the executive officer exclaimed as the first of the 1,400 Allied strike force ships approached the strait heading for several port cities of North Africa.

"We can't help them!"

Adnet and team 1 heard the large formation of C-47 aircraft. They were on schedule and on course to drop thousands of paratroopers behind the German defense lines 5 miles inland. Adnet expected the aircraft as part of Operation Husky and the invasion of Sicily. The first wave of aircraft disgorged the many white parachutes and made a large sweeping turn to return to Tunis to complete their part of the operation. There were to be three waves of paratroopers in the coming hours. Adnet and team 1 left for their assigned trip to Southern Greece before the second and third flights.

They later learned the second and third waves were not as successful. Friendly fire destroyed many of the aircraft.

Unfortunately, the French resistance and team 1 were well clear of the area before most of the friendly fire erupted. They could have saved many of the paratroopers but were ordered to proceed north. They were to board a transport to Southern Greece.

"Should we report it to headquarters?" Blake asked.

"Probably hundreds of other reports will be made, and more troops are expected later to help recover lost soldiers," Adnet responded. "Let's get going, we can't help, and we need to be in Sardinia by late tomorrow."

Chapter 30

ABOARD THE MANCHESTER

"That was more excitement than I had bargained for." Blake said as he addressed Nate and Martinez. "Those ropes were cold and slick. The only reason I continued to climb is that I didn't want to get my letter from Vivian wet."

"I hope that is all the excitement we experience." Martinez said while recovering from the climb up the side of the cruiser.

As the three men huddled at the railing of the ship, a familiar officer approached. "Good to see you again," Lieutenant Commander Morrison said as he shook the outstretched hands of the three men. "I trust you had an interesting transfer to the ship. That will teach you to be more prompt to your appointments. We waited at the dock as long as we could."

"Good to see you too, but you need to work on your elevator. I don't care for the makeshift rope ladder you provided us," Blake said. "We won't miss any appointments in the future. That was scary for us flat-landers."

"Let's find your quarters and get you some food. I bet you are hungry, and I can tell that you need a shower," Morrison said. "Welcome aboard, gentlemen, and you too, Nate. Please follow me." Blake and Martinez giggled at the affront to poor Nate.

"We are to attend a briefing at 1800 hours. That gives you enough time to shower and get into some clean fatigues. I will take you to the mess at 1630 hours just before the briefing." Morrison directed.

The briefing started promptly at 1800 hours and ended exactly twelve minutes later. The mission: to shadow a wolf pack of German and Italian submarines as they move south along the coast of Morocco. It was the same wolf pack that blockaded the Strait of Gibraltar just hours earlier. We are to record their movements until the strike force has passed through the strait and enters the Mediterranean. We were not to engage but watch and report to the strike force as they approach the ports of Oran and Algiers.

"I thought we would see some action on this trip. It's nothing but seawater and seasickness," Blake said while drinking more soda water to settle his stomach. "I would rather be placing more camel dung covers in the desert and die of dehydration rather than loose bowels and vomiting. It just isn't a proper way to fight a war."

Chapter 31

THE GENERAL DISAPPEARS

A large group of C-47 transports sailed effortlessly through the dark cloudless skies of the Northern Mediterranean Sea heading for Sicily. It was past midnight on July 11, 1943. The general on board one of the planes felt the flight was safe from enemy fire. The group was scheduled to return before dawn the following morning. He ignored his directive to remain in Tunisia to support later flights to Sicily and wanted to follow the action in Sicily. Taking the final flight of C-47s was to deposit more paratroopers behind enemy lines and should be safe.

The path of the flight flew directly over the Allied naval fleet positioned off the coast of Southern Sicily. The plan was to drop several thousand paratroopers behind German defenses and return to Malta by sunrise. Operation Husky was the extension of the Operation Torch intended to land Allied forces on the shores of Sicily. The general reasoned that it should be safe for the C-47s to fly over the Allied armada, deposit the paratroopers, and return to Malta without incident. Unfortunately, the armada of ships had just been strafed by German fighters and bombers as the group of C-47s approached. A gunner aboard one of the ships, thinking the planes were German bombers, opened fire on the C-47s, and in unison, many other gunners joined in firing on the C-47s loaded with Allied paratroopers.

That night, twenty-three of the aircraft were either destroyed or damaged and forced to ditch in the Mediterranean. Most of the paratroopers either lost their lives by jumping out of the C-47s before attaching their parachutes or drowned in the water. Many of the paratroopers were shot while descending from the C-47s.

The general's aircraft was hit several times and forced to ditch off the coast of Sicily. Several of the crew and the general were able to swim the 400 yards to the beach and began searching the beach for other crew members. The general found himself alone on the beach. A sergeant from another flight downed by the friendly fire approached the general, but no other members of the crew were found and assumed drowned.

The general was determined to join the other paratroopers dropped behind the enemy lines. He left the beach and headed inland. The sergeant later tried to find the general, but he had disappeared. No trace of him was ever found.

Chapter 32

Team 2, Dino and Enzo, in Arta, Greece

"Where is Echo?" Dino asked.

"Where he belongs, down below with Nora to keep him quiet," Enzo explained. The dog was to remain silent as their boat neared the rendezvous at Arta. The village was slightly inland in a natural estuary and usually safe from Axis forces.

It was different this time. The last time Enzo had been here, there were a few Italian forces, but now there were German forces everywhere. Luca was to meet them and help them find their quarters inland while avoiding the German patrols.

"The Germans have moved many divisions of troops and supporting personnel and equipment to the islands of Corsica and Sardinia from Sicily and Italy in the last two weeks," Luca explained. "They must be expecting the Allies to attack there very soon. I've been told there are now eighteen divisions of German troops in the two Italian islands."

"I wonder why so many of the German troops moved from Sicily just before the Allied attack in Operation Husky," Dino wondered to John. "It is like the Germans planned for the Allied invasion at Greece and Crete instead of Sicily."

"Just bad planning, I guess," John responded.

"No, they moved for a reason," Dino said. "They never move without a reason."

Nate wants what?

Chapter 33

FRENCH RESISTANCE VERSUS GERMAN TANKS

"Get me some flaked or powdered soap," Nate ordered while describing a device the resistance could use against the Vichy French and German tanks as they move across the southern part of France. "This should discourage the tanks from moving freely against local resistance."

"Why do you want soap?" Adnet asked in frustration. "We need something to stop the tanks, not clean their clothes."

"This will do more than clean their clothes," Nate continued. "If this works, it will make the tanks intolerably hot. It will raise the temperature in the tanks or burn through portions of the tank to consume the occupants. They will have to get out of the tanks or burn. When they leave the safety of the tanks, you will be there with your rifles to make sure they don't continue to fight."

"What else do you need?"

"Some sawdust would be perfect, but dried grasses will also work," Nate added. "The trick is to make a slurry that will burn hot for more than a few seconds."

"Is it a Molotov cocktail?"

"No, it's more like a napalm cocktail," Nate said. "We can throw the cocktail or set a fuse to ignite it from a safe distance . . ." Nate paused while thinking. "Oh yeah, I'll need some black grease and old socks. I also need more of the land mines that we used in North Africa. Instead of using camel dung as a disguise, we will use clumps of native grasses or rock-shaped covers."

"Who will throw the cocktails?" Adnet asked, concerned for the safety of his men.

"Sergeant Martinez will train your men, but we will all have to the place the mines and throw the cocktails," Nate explained. "Now go get the supplies I need to complete the cocktails."

"Haven't you forgotten the ingredient that makes the cocktails burn?" Adnet asked.

"Yes, you and your men will have to borrow gasoline, diesel fuel, and kerosene from the Vichy French or Germans," Nate answered.

"How much will you need, and where can we store and assemble the cocktails?" Adnet asked as he finished the supply list they needed.

"Get as much as you think we can take without creating suspicion. One last thing—" Nate said. "If you can find some old cast iron casing material and soot, I can make some coal bombs."

"What are coal bombs?" Adnet asked while preparing to leave for his hunting expedition.

"Coal bombs were used by the Confederacy during the American Civil War. They were designed to explode in a coal-burning furnace. They were introduced to disable steam-driven ships and railroad engines. The cast iron casing was shaped like coal and coated with soot to resemble coal then filled with gunpowder that exploded in the furnace," Nate explained. "The furnaces were damaged beyond repair and often caused damage to the steam boilers and would explode. Several ships were disabled for long periods for needed repairs."

"Okay, I'll go now. Please, no more needed items. I will have to find a place to hide all this stuff. For now, this old house will hide your team. I will return tonight, after midnight."

Nate went downstairs of the old house where Martinez and Blake were busy working out plans for their stay in Agde in Southern France. "What's for dinner tonight? I'm starving."

"Black grease and old socks," Blake said with a smile. "What have you been selling the resistance, and how will you detonate those things?"

"That's the tricky part. We will have to steal gasoline from the Germans," Nate continued. "Kerosene or diesel fuel burn more slowly but will work if we can't find gasoline. Fuses or vials of nitro would work nicely."

"How much will we need, and where we are going to store it?"

"Adnet is working on it."

"There are two more items we will need, but you will have to ask Alsos Headquarters for them. We will need some iron castings and soot to make the coal bombs."

"Oh, is that all? Why don't you order some hamburgers and beer while you're at it?"

"Great idea. Make mine a green chili hamburger and a Coors, and don't forget the cheese," Nate answered with a grin. "You will also have to order glass vials of nitro and phosphorous plus some dynamite fuses."

"I hope you know what you are doing, our resistance partners could hurt themselves using that stuff," Blake continued. "I have no idea what a coal bomb is or a sticky bomb, but I bet they will be nasty, and I hope you explained what they are and how they work to Adnet."

"What about more camel dung mine covers and poison sumac?" Martinez asked while working on an attack plan for the resistance. "I will be able to train them on most items, but the nitro and phosphorous vials are out of my league."

"Don't worry, I will help with the training. The mine covers will have to be different since there are no camels in Southern France. The same goes for the poison sumac. The plant is not indigenous to the area, and we would be in violation of the Geneva Convention."

"Aren't we supposed to report enemy activity and not get directly involved in the war? Now we're involved up to our necks."

"Are you afraid of getting your hands dirty?"

"No, but I would prefer to return home with my hands instead of having them blown off by a charge of some unknown stuff."

Chapter 34

TEAM 2 LANDS IN SICILY

The British submarine *Endeavor* stopped at midnight on November 12, off the coast of Sicily, near the small fishing village of Butera.

"Your ride awaits you," the executive officer said as John and Dino were ushered forward onto the deck of the submarine. "The Italian underground should arrive any minute and are gracious enough to provide transportation for your trip."

"Great, we're working with the Italian resistance again," John said. "Colonel Powers said team 1 will join us for a briefing tomorrow. I wonder if Davis and Martinez will also join us."

"It will be the first time both teams will work together," Dino added. "Must be big. Do you think the invasion of Italy is likely?"

"The invasion of Italy is imminent," John said. "I think it all depends on whether the Vichy French and the Italians continue to support the Nazi occupation of their countries. Mussolini has lost favor with the king and Italian people, especially since Hitler demanded another 250,000 Italian troops be sent to the Eastern Front and sure death at the hands of the advancing Russians. It may be a matter of time before the Italian forces join the Allies to drive the Nazis out of Italy."

Enzo maneuvered the small boat alongside the submarine as John and Dino scrambled to join him for the short trip to the shoreline. "Get aboard quickly!" Enzo exclaimed. "Patrol boats have been watching all traffic on the beach. Why is it that I always have to move you guys around in the dark when German patrols are in the area?"

"You're just lucky," John said. "It's good to see you too."

As the submarine disappeared beneath the waters off Sicily, a dark fog began to form around the small boat heading for the shoreline. In the darkness, there was no sound but the sound of the small boat motor. Enzo shut off the small engine as they drew close to the dock and told John and Dino to work the oars for the short distance to the dock. It was so quiet John heard the sound of his heart beating in his ears, like the sound of a man walking fast on hard ground.

"Toss the line to Luca," Enzo whispered.

Luca tied off the small boat. The oars were replaced as Nora and Echo approached the dock.

Echo jumped aboard the boat and into the waiting arms of Dino. Echo began whining and licking the face of Dino at the same time beating his hard tail into the back of John.

"Shut him up!" Enzo ordered.

"It's all right," Nora explained. "There are no patrol boats in the area, and the village is quiet. I think he likes you. What did you do to earn his affection?"

"Nothing," Dino explained. "I just played with him while we were running silently from our last trip. Dogs and women are just naturally attracted to me."

"The only things attracted to you are an occasional head cold and house flies," John added jokingly.

Muted laughter erupted as everyone jumped onto the dock. "Hurry! Follow me. We're ordered to a briefing at 0600 hours," Enzo ordered.

Chapter 35

WHAT DOES NATE WANT NOW?

"Another weird request just came in from Nate," the radio operator said as he handed the note to Colonel Powers.

"What does he want now? Is it another cover for one of his firecrackers?"

"No, sir. It sounds much more dangerous. He has asked for dynamite fuses and vials of nitro and phosphorous. What should I do with his request?"

"I'll handle it," Powers said as he took the request and headed for the Office of Strategic Services next door. The OSS was involved with many of the projects needed by Alsos and other branches of the army to stop or slow the advancing Axis forces in North Africa.

* * *

"Good morning, Colonel Powers." The sergeant stood at attention as Powers entered the OSS office. "What can I do for you?"

"Looking for Captain Townsend. Is he in his laboratory?"

"Yes, sir. Should I let him know you are here?"

"No, thanks. I'll find him."

Townsend was studying recent aerial photographs and maps as Powers approached. Unaware of Powers's presence, Townsend was mumbling to himself as he studied the maps and photographs spread across his desk.

"Why have the Germans abandoned the Strait of Gibraltar? Months of planning and movement of supplies and personnel into the area to control the strait, and now moving everything out. What are they doing? Is this a repeat of Operation Sea Lion where months of preparation to attack England were abandoned at the last minute? I wonder what they called the operation to control the Strait of Gibraltar. Had the operation succeeded, it would have closed the Mediterranean to Allied shipping to North Africa, ensuring Axis control of the region."

Powers was listening to Townsend's mumbling and finally interrupted during a pause. "It was Felix."

Townsend jumped at the interruption, turned to find Powers standing a few feet away. "Sorry, sir, I didn't hear you come in."

"How are you, Captain? Sorry to disturb your thoughts, but I thought you knew the name of the Axis operation to control the strait."

Townsend stood at attention and finally regained his senses. "You scared the hell out of me, sir. And no, I didn't know the name of the operation."

"The name of the operation is secret. We don't want the Germans to know how we got the information."

"How did you learn about Felix before my office?"

"Sorry, Captain, that information is well above your pay grade," Powers continued. "My office must have a few secrets of our own."

"I'm sure you haven't ventured into my lab to discuss names of German operations," Townsend said. "What can I do for you, Colonel?"

"Do you recall the request team 2 made about the camel dung mine covers?"

"Of course. How could I forget such a weird request and the great way it worked to slow the German tanks?"

"Team 1 is now asking for sticky bombs and coal torpedoes or coal bombs."

"That's new to me. What is a sticky bomb or a coal bomb?"

"A sticky bomb is an old sock full of explosives covered in grease or pitch that will stick the side of a tank then detonate."

"How does it detonate?"

"That's why I'm here. The team plans to use a fuse to light before throwing or placing on the side of a tank," Powers continued. "We were hoping you would have a better way to detonate the bombs."

"The coal bomb, I remember from my Civil War history, but I don't know much about it, except that it involved metal casings and gunpowder," Townsend continued. "The coal bomb was self-detonating, while the sticky bomb will need a detonator or fuse."

"That's correct!" Powers injected. "We need a detonator for the sticky bomb and a better design for the coal bomb, a design that includes high explosives instead of gunpowder."

"Sounds like you need something to throw at the tanks from a safe distance. You also need something to place in coal bins to destroy coal-burning furnaces or steam engines like trains or coal burning ships."

"Can you shape dynamite into a lump of coal?"

"I can check it out. We will have to paint it black, but I think we can do it."

"That would solve our problem with the coal bomb. What about a detonator for the sticky bomb?"

"Maybe something that would detonate when it struck the tank. My first thought was nitroglycerin or perhaps phosphorous, but I will need to do some studying before I can say it will work. Both materials are dangerous to handle. You could disable more handlers than German tanks."

"Nate mentioned both materials in his request," Powers continued. "Nate was in the navy several years back and may be familiar with the materials from his training. Can they use locally-made napalm in the sticky bomb?" Powers asked.

"I can't imagine them producing napalm while working with the resistance. They would need gasoline and soap mixed to form a thick slurry. Dangerous to handle by untrained personnel, but yes, it can be made in the field."

"Could we use a form of phosphorous, such as a nitride or a sulfide?" Powers asked.

"Still volatile and dangerous to handle. I would not even try using any of the phosphorous products due to safety concerns. I doubt the Geneva Convention would approve either."

"How about the nitroglycerin?"

"Too dangerous to handle."

"Can you shape dynamite like a lump of coal?"

"If you are talking about shaping dynamite to look like coal, yes, that might work and be safer for the resistance to use. I'll have to check it out before I commit to shaping dynamite safely."

"Can you have something for me in three days?" Colonel Powers asked on his way out of Townsend's office. "Let me know SOON, the resistance needs it now. They are planning to disable two troop transport trains moving to Southern Greece and to stuff in the barrels of the German artillery."

Chapter 36

Colonel Powers's Concerns

Colonel Powers left the OSS laboratory to return to the routine of his office. He was concerned about his plans. He needed time to think and did not want to return to the office and the constant interruptions. He felt the need for solitude to think. He decided to walk to a small sidewalk café several blocks from his office, hoping that few patrons would be dining this early in the morning. The walk of several blocks helped calm his busy brain, and he found a table away from a small group of patrons at the café.

The issues he wanted to resolve were personal but effected his teams working with the French and Italian resistance. The first was to find a means to keep his teams safe in fast-changing battles and movements of Axis and Allied troops. The second was his inability to control the next moves of all the various combatants in the conflict. Constant change and the fluid actions were not as predictable as he liked. Few promises were kept on either side of the war, and many of the orders and comments were designed to deceive.

After ordering a cup of hot coffee, Powers began to make notes of the issues:

1. Part of Operation Torch counted on the Vichy French forces in Morocco and Tunisia to join the Allies to help push the

Axis forces out of North Africa. The exiled Free French government in London headed by General De Gaulle held little to no support of the Vichy French in North Africa. Relations between the French and British were cold again. The Allied commander could not count on French support and would possibly mean killing French soldiers besides Axis forces.

2. Sabotage by night landings of German paratroopers in Free French- and Vichy French-occupied areas of North Africa forced the Allies to rely on the few Free French forces to guard hundreds of culverts, bridges, tunnels, and communication lines. Still, the Free French forces were reluctant to help.

3. Both of his teams in North Africa and now in Sicily and Greece had to deal with teams of forces with unknown or changing loyalties. Italian and German troops were occupying Italian areas and, in some areas, fighting Italian resistance.

4. What were the Germans thinking when they first bombed then attacked Tunisia where the Vichy French forces dominated? Then the Germans began invading Southern France held by Vichy French forces. These tactics forced the Vichy and Free French forces to join the Allies, at least in France.

5. General Patton's involvement in Morocco either killed or pushed the Vichy French eastward, while the Germans bombed Tunis. This forced the Vichy and Free French to support the Allies.

6. Was it a miscalculation by German High Command to attack Tunisia at the expense of Vichy French support? Was it British or underground propaganda that convinced the Axis forces to invade Southern France and Tunisia?

7. Whatever the reason, 250,000 German and Italian soldiers retreated to Tunis and forced to surrender by the pincher action of American forces from the west and the British from the east.

After several cups of coffee, two bathroom breaks, and a meat pie, Powers felt better about his chances to keep his teams safe.

Powers returned to his office to find Townsend sitting in his office, reading.

"Miss your lunch?" Powers asked as he took his seat behind the desk.

"Yes, sir, thought you would like a quick answer to your questions you asked this morning. I have some good news and some bad. Which would you prefer first?"

"Give me the bad news first."

"Actually, there isn't any bad news. It will just take a little more time to get your supplies put together . . ." Townsend paused as the colonel frowned at the mention of more time needed. "I have ordered the dynamite to be shaped like coal and thermite grenades to replace your sticky bombs."

"Thermite grenades? We hadn't thought of that. They would be safer to handle and much quieter. They could be placed without being heard or seen."

"It will be necessary to place the grenades in the artillery barrels and tanks when they are not in use. They will disable the barrels or the recoil and traversing mechanisms. If the resistance can place the grenades on or under the tank tracks, the 4,500-degree temperature will melt and weaken the tracks. They will fail either immediately or shortly after they begin using them."

"What do you think?"

"What about the napalm for the sticky bomb?"

"Not recommended for use by the resistance or our personnel. They are dangerous, noisy, and highly visible. The noise and fire would alert the enemy of their position . . ." Townsend paused while both men were digesting the information. "The 155mm artillery pieces can be silenced with the thermite grenade if placed either in the recoil mechanism or the barrel. The guns would be dangerous to fire and likely explode or bend the barrel to disrupt the aiming function. "The thermite grenades are ideal for use by the resistance. They can be placed at night in the dark by a single man or two-men teams, especially those placed in the barrels of the artillery. The light is minimal, they make no noise and not likely to alert the enemy."

"When can I expect to receive the thermite grenades and coal bombs?"

"They are on the way as we speak. I still have some of the mine covers that can be shipped to the teams, if you think they can use them."

"Send them too."

Chapter 37

TWO MEN ON THEIR BELLIES

Two men waited for the moon to fade by the thin clouds before moving toward the Italian tanks.

"Stay in the ditch and keep your head down," Sergeant Martinez ordered as he and Adnet waited for the opportunity to use the thermite grenades.

"I know—stay in the ditch, be quiet, and watch for the guards. If the guards come within 30 yards of you, key the radio twice but don't say anything."

"Well, I'll be damned, you can remember instruction," Martinez responded while watching the fast-moving clouds overhead. "This will be a good first test of the grenades. We didn't have to make use of the sticky bombs, and the grenades should be safer."

"Should I create a diversion if the guards come too close to you?" Adnet asked.

"No, stay quiet and out of sight. Just key the radio. I will silence the radio but will hear the clicks. The last thing we want is to alert the Axis forces we are operating in their area."

"How long will you be gone?"

"I'll place two thermite grenades under two of the tank tracks and should be back in forty minutes."

"Why so long?"

"I'll have to dig under the tracks and cover the tracks with sand to silence any sound, light, and smoke of the grenades. Shouldn't be any sound or light under the tank, but there will be some smoke that will escape from under the tracks," Martinez answered. "Then crawl back here. It will take a good thirty or forty minutes."

"How will you detonate the grenades?"

"I will stay with one of the grenades and attach a string to the pull pin on the second grenade, pull both pins at the same time, and run like the wind."

Suddenly, the clouds covered the moon, and Martinez was on his belly, crawling toward the first Italian tank 60 yards away. He felt sure the sound of the thermite grenade would be muted by the tank track and sand. The 4,500 degrees of heat produced by the grenade would partially melt the track, while the sound would be more of a sizzle than a blast.

Martinez reached the first tank before the clouds parted to expose the moon. He felt relieved, but the threat of bright moonlight would expose his position. He began to dig the first hole with the small spade he brought with him. He remained on his belly, staying as quiet as possible. There was no sound from the tank or from any of the guards nearby.

It was hard to believe that a small thermite grenade could disable the massive piece of Italian iron that loomed above. He placed the grenade in a position under the tank track but in contact with the underside of the track. He filled the hole with sand but left the grenade pull pin exposed until he could attach a string between the two grenades. By using the string, he could pull the pins at the same time to allow him to escape.

Still no noise. The moon obscured by the clouds. Everything was going as planned.

Suddenly, he heard two clicks on his radio. He quickly crawled under the second tank, hoping the guard would pass by without stopping. He could not hear any sound but was sure Adnet had seen a guard approach his position. A few seconds later, he heard the voices of two guards.

Then he heard the footsteps, more of a shuffling in the dirt and sand. The guards were not trying to be quiet. Their laughter and the kidding of each other could be easily heard. They passed quickly and continued toward the guard shack located about 70 yards beyond the tanks.

Martinez returned to his digging under the track of the first tank after taking several deep breaths to control his nerves. He finished placing the first grenade and crawled to the second tank, thankful the moon had not reappeared through the clouds. He ran the cord along his side as he crawled the 5 yards to the next target.

Before he could reach the second tank, the clouds opened to expose the bright moon and his cord running between the tanks. He quickly moved under the tank to stay out of sight.

Adnet keyed the radio twice again as one of the guards stepped out of the guard shack and moved toward the tanks.

Fortunately, the guard's only interest was in relieving his bladder. From his position, the guard was scanning the area and noticed the cord strung between the front two tanks. Without hesitation, he shouted to the other guard that he was going to check the cord.

Martinez froze at the alert from Adnet. He could see the feet of the guard approaching, but there was nothing he could do to conceal the cord or move away from the tank.

Just as the guard approached the cord, there was a loud sound of glass breaking and the painful shout of the second guard. The guard stopped, turned, and ran back to the guard shack to find the second guard covered with sharp shards of dirty glass and bleeding from open contusions of his head and face.

Adnet had thrown the stone to distract the guard approaching Martinez. In the confusion, he ran quickly to the second tank and joined Martinez under the tank instead of trying to hide or escape down the ditch. Within seconds, both guards were searching the ditch with bright flashlights. Adnet was correct to think that they would look for the stone thrower in the ditch. The distraction allowed the two saboteurs time to detonate the two grenades and escape to the opposite side of the tank column.

"I thought I told you to stay in the ditch, stay quiet, and no diversions," Martinez chided Adnet sarcastically.

"You could thank me for saving your butt," Adnet argued.

"That was a great shot to hit the window from that distance, but don't do it again. We could have both been caught and shot."

"Let's do it again with a couple of supply trucks."

"No, not tonight," Martinez said. "Let's not press our luck. We could have been caught or shot if the guards had found us. Let's wait for an opportunity less likely to get us killed."

The next morning the two lead tanks in the column of ten tanks started to move but quickly lost a track. It took four hours and a repair team of five men to repair the tanks, delaying the intended mission of the Italian tanks. Ten tanks were disabled before an unknown battle.

Chapter 38

TRAINING THE RESISTANCE

"Do you think the other members of the resistance know how to use the devices?" Martinez asked.

"Sure. I do have a couple of questions though," Adnet said. "Why avoid water while using the thermite grenades? Oh yeah, why covers on the land mines to look like cow dung?"

"The land mines must be disguised, or the tank commanders will just steer around them. A small clump of grass or gravel placed over the mines will conceal some of the mines. But if the tank drivers suspect anything, they will avoid them," Martinez continued. "If the grass or gravel won't work, use the cow-dung covers because they love to spray following tanks and soldiers with the suspected manure. To answer your other question, the thermite grenades produce a very high temperature fire and will explode with metal fragments that continue to burn if exposed to water," Martinez explained. "Be very careful with them."

Chapter 39

TEAM 2 REASSIGNED

"Forget Sardinia," Colonel Powers instructed team 2. "The Axis forces have moved sixteen to eighteen divisions to Sardinia and Corsica, leaving only two divisions of German forces to assist the Italians in Sicily."

"Okay, where do you want us to go?" Dino asked. "Are the Italian resistance to move also?"

"You and the Italian resistance will be moved to the northwest area of Sicily to monitor Axis troop movements. Generals Patton and Montgomery will be pushing up the east and west coasts toward Messina in hopes of capturing the Axis troops before they can escape to the mainland by way of the Messina Strait."

"We just received the shipment of thermite grenades and land mines, what should we do with them?" Dino asked. "Leave them or take them with us?"

"Leave them for Adnet and his men. Your team will receive more, if needed," Powers continued. "You, John, and Enzo will move by fishing boat to a point 40 miles west of Messina. You will be met by a British MI6 agent with further instructions."

"Yes, sir," Dino answered.

John and Enzo overheard the radio message and sat perplexed about the recent change. "Messina will be a dangerous place with retreating Axis troops flooding the area and General Patton pushing Allied forces after them," John finally said. "I hope Powers made some arrangements to keep us safe."

"Powers has taken good care of us before, that shouldn't change," Dino injected while he and Enzo checked maps of the landing site.

"I'll send Luca ahead tonight to check the area," Enzo added.

"I wonder which MI6 agent will meet us?" John asked. "Maybe it will be Murphy. I would like to see her again."

Chapter 40

Italian Patrol Boat

"Get rid of your weapons and Italian papers!" Enzo whispered as an Italian patrol boat came into site with their lights teamed on the fishing boat. "If asked, give them your Japanese papers and don't speak."

John and Dino followed the orders of Enzo and quietly slipped their Italian papers under a loose board in the bow of the boat while dropping their two Colt 45s into the water.

"Kill your engine. Place your hands on your heads. Present your papers and explain what you are doing in these waters," the Italian lieutenant ordered.

"Yes, sir," Enzo said while motioning for John and Dino to place their hands on their heads. Both men spoke Italian and pretended to be Japanese.

The officer was curious about the Japanese papers of John and Dino and waiting for an explanation from Enzo.

"I am an Italian security officer taking these two Japanese doctors to the lighted dock off your port bough. They have been placed in my care from a German submarine 5 miles out to sea," Enzo explained. "They are meeting Gen. Giovanni Messa to be taken to the aircraft plant near Messina."

"What aircraft plant?" the lieutenant asked while pointing his weapon at Enzo.

"It is a new aircraft plant a few miles inland from Messina," Enzo explained.

"I know nothing of an aircraft plant near Messina. I must contact my supervisor for instructions. Wait here until I clear your passage. Do the doctors speak Italian?"

"No, only Japanese. We must hurry to meet General Messa, he is a very impatient man," Enzo explained. "The general wants us to be in the facility before dawn and out of sight. We must hurry!"

"You must wait until I contact my supervisor," the lieutenant said in frustration.

"I understand," Enzo said. "However, I doubt General Messa will understand why you are interfering. I hope he will agree with you rather than having you shot. Our destination is just there at the lighted dock. It is not far, and I will put in a good word for you when we reach the general. What is your name and rank? Give me your supervisor's name, and I will mention that you helped us meet the general."

"Please, I must contact my supervisor."

"Does your supervisor wish to disappoint the general too?" Enzo asked. "If not, stop wasting our time and return our papers!"

"Okay, I will escort you to the dock. Here are your papers." The lieutenant finally conceded. "What is the name of the general again? I am not familiar with him?"

Chapter 41

GENERAL, WHO?

Dressed in dark clothing, Maj. Murphy Donnelly of MI6 waited patiently on the lighted fishing dock for team 2. "Where are they? Fifty minutes late. It will be dawn soon."

She stopped pacing around the dock as she heard an approaching boat. Unfortunately, the small fishing boat was accompanied by an Italian patrol boat. In the early morning darkness, she could identify the fishing boat, but why was a patrol boat following them? Has the team been taken into custody? Something is wrong.

Donnelly wanted to run and hide or anything but stay and confront the Italian patrol, but that wouldn't help the team. Instead, she stood her ground to see what was happening.

As the two boats approached the dock, two armed Italian soldiers jumped onto the dock with their weapons pointed at Murphy. "Put your hands on your head."

Murphy did as she was told. "What is the meaning of this?" Murphy asked in impeccable Italian.

Just as quickly, Enzo jumped onto the dock and came to the side of Murphy. "Where is General Messa? He was to meet us here."

Murphy quickly replied in confusion. "I was told to meet you. I guess the general was delayed."

Enzo introduced Murphy to the two Japanese aeronautical scientists then asked, "How are we to get to the research facility?"

"Who are you and let me see your papers?" the Italian lieutenant ordered.

As Murphy passed her papers to the lieutenant, she tried to explain who she was and why she was there instead of the general. The lieutenant returned her papers and wanted to know about her job. "I'm a typist in supply. I was ordered to pick up two people at the dock, but I don't know why the general was delayed. All I know is that we must leave before dawn."

Enzo then ordered the team to move toward their transport and began moving toward the end of the pier and out of site. The confused Italian soldiers stood in misbelief as the party disappeared.

"Don't forget to put in a good word for me to the general," the Italian lieutenant mentioned as the party moved away.

"Keep moving," Murphy ordered. "They won't shoot us in the back, at least I hope not."

Chapter 42

WHO IS GENERAL MESSA?

Team 2 followed Murphy as they moved away from the Italian patrol. The encounter ended much better than any of them imagined. John, Dino, and Enzo were still sweating bullets as they climbed into the transport to take them to the secret nonexistent research facility.

"I'm glad the Italian patrol didn't follow us to see the vehicle we are taking to the research facility," John said. "It doesn't look like a proper vehicle for a general. More like an Italian farmer. Where did you find the hay and goats?"

"Don't ask," Murphy answered. "I had no idea I was supposed to be a general's driver."

"If Enzo hadn't come to me before the Italian lieutenant and mentioned the general, we would probably be in prison now or facing a firing squad," Murphy said. "Who is this general?"

"Don't worry, he does exist, but he is currently busy on the Eastern Front at Hitler's request," Enzo explained. "I would be surprised if he answers his telephone where he is. In fact, he probably won't answer a telephone ever again. I will put in a good word for the Italian lieutenant if I ever see the general. His supervisor may have him shot if he finds out that he let us pass. I would bet that his supervisor will not hear of the incident. I know I would keep it to myself if it were me."

John finally greeted Murphy. "Good to see you again. Maybe we can find another cantina for a drink like we did in Malta. You have saved our butts again from Axis troops."

"Why are you always being chased by bad guys or in some kind of trouble?" Murphy asked.

"It's the only way I get to see you," John answered.

"This time I will be driving, while you and Dino will ride in the back. Enzo will be in the front with me. Don't ask any questions, just get under the hay, and leave the goats alone."

"Why can't Dino and I drive while you and Enzo ride in the back?" John suggested while moving the tick-infested goats and smelly hay.

"Because I outrank you, and I'm allergic to hay, and not to mention, you don't know where you are or where we are going," Murphy explained.

"But our orders are to watch for retreating Axis forces headed toward Messina and the strait," John tried to reason.

"My orders are to keep you alive and out of trouble. Now let me do my job. Get under the hay, or I'll shoot you myself."

"Yes, madam or Major. I'll try to be good. Where are we going?"

"One of several old buildings which have a view of the eastern coastline and the road leading to Messina," Murphy answered.

"That road will be busy," Dino added. "Thousands of Axis forces being chased by thousands of American soldiers. If we are to delay the Axis forces heading to Messina in retreat, we will need some help," Dino went on.

"Let's wait to see what your orders are before we panic and call in the Calvary," Murphy suggested.

"We will need a disinfectant and hot shower," Dino said while covering his lower body with hay. "We will also need a good sauce to cook this goat if he doesn't stop trying to butt me."

"Leave her alone," Enzo added. "She's my favorite goat. She just likes you, but I can't imagine why."

"Get under the hay," Murphy ordered as they drove off.

Chapter 43

HILL 027

"It will be dawn soon. We must be out of sight before dawn," Murphy explained to team 2, still on the road to the old farmhouse.

"A truck is coming!" Enzo shouted.

"What is it?" Murphy asked as they proceeded in the dark. "I can't tell yet. Get completely under the hay!" she shouted to John and Dino.

"It's a German patrol. Keep driving slowly unless they force us to stop," Enzo said.

"They have stopped in the road and motioning for us to stop. Keep moving and just wave as a couple of Italian farm workers going to market."

As the old truck passed the German patrol, it was evident they wanted the truck to stop. A friendly wave from Murphy and Enzo did not please the officer riding in the sidecar of the motorcycle.

"They have turned around and following us with their lights flashing."

"How is your German?" Murphy asked Enzo.

"Not good."

"Just pretend to be asleep."

Murphy slowed the truck, tapped the brakes, and stopped the old truck as if to allow the patrol to pass.

The patrol stopped behind the truck, keeping their lights concentrated on the truck.

Murphy had withdrawn her pistol from under her seat and held it ready in her right hand but out of sight while leaving her left hand on the wheel.

The motorcycle was one of those with a sidecar where the officer sat, while the third rider sat higher behind the driver and yielded an automatic rifle.

The German officer dismounted and approached the front of the truck while waving a German Luger in the general direction of Murphy.

"Good morning," Murphy said in Italian. "What is wrong?" she asked while preparing to shoot the officer through the door.

"What are you doing, and where are you going?" the German officer asked in Italian. "Give me your papers."

"We are taking my goats to Messina market for sale," Murphy said while passing their papers to the officer.

"Are you carrying anything else?" the officer asked while motioning for the motorcycle driver to check the back of the truck, Leaving the soldier and his automatic rifle still pointed in the direction of the truck.

"No, just goats and hay to sell in Messina."

The soldier told to check the back of the truck was reluctantly climbing aboard the truck. He dropped back to the ground using the slats on the side of the truck. One of the larger goats kept butting him as he tried to climb over the top slat.

The German officer checked their papers, found them correct, and returned them to Murphy. "What's the matter with your friend there?" the officer asked.

"Nothing, just too much to drink last night."

That seemed to satisfy the officer and then turned to focus his attention on the soldier trying to climb into the back of the truck. "What's wrong with you, afraid of a little goat?"

"They have horns, and the big one keeps butting me," the soldier replied.

"Just stick your rifle through the slats into the hay to see if they are carrying anything else," the officer ordered.

As the soldier tried to stick his rifle through the slats, the larger goat attacked the approaching rifle barrel. He butted the rifle several times, forcing the soldier to withdraw his rifle.

"If there were more people in the hay, that goat would have killed them," the soldier said, hoping the officer would agree to leave the goat alone.

Murphy pleaded with the officer to leave the goat alone. Enzo had appeared to be awakened by the noise and joined in the pleading. The German officer was becoming increasingly frustrated by the pleading of the farmers and the soldier. He was waving his Lugar at Murphy and Enzo and shouting at the soldier fighting the goat.

"Shoot the damn goat!" the German officer ordered.

Before the soldier could raise his weapon to shoot the goat, Enzo tossed a hand grenade over the top of the cab of the truck into the empty sidecar of the motorcycle.

The explosion sent shrapnel into the bodies of the soldier behind the truck and the machine-gun operator still on the motorcycle. The officer avoided direct impact of the explosion but was stunned but uninjured. Before he could regain his senses, Murphy shot him through the door.

In panic, Murphy drove the truck away from the site. "Won't this thing go any faster?" She was concerned that the Italian patrol boat had heard the gunfire and would be investigating.

John and Dino had remained under the hay through the explosion and gunfire and were told to remain there until the team reached the farmhouse where they could dispose of the truck.

When the team reached the house on Hill 027 John and Dino finally climbed down from the back of the truck to find that two of the goats had been killed by flying shrapnel. Fortunately, the goat that had been doing all the butting was in perfect health. As Dino stepped down from the truck, he said, "We won't be needing the sauce to cook the goat. I think I will kiss him instead. He helped save our butts with his butts."

Chapter 44

TWO DISABLED TANKS

Nate and Blake had been working on reports to Alsos Headquarters but stopped to add some comments about the results of the two saboteurs' actions from the night before.

"Nice work," Nate said. "You disabled two tanks, but you could have blown a supply truck or two instead of running and hiding."

"Easy for you to say," Martinez said in defense of their actions. "While you play on the radio and write reports, we could have been captured or killed."

"We thought it best for the German guards to think a couple of kids threw the rock instead of two saboteurs," Adnet added.

"Good thinking," Blake said. "The Germans would have been alerted of our presence and started searching for us."

"Just a couple of sissies," Nate joked.

"Were you able to disguise the thermite grenades? Do we need to change the way we place the grenades?" Blake asked.

"We placed them under and in contact with the tracks and covered them with about six inches of sand. The light and sound were not noticeable, but we couldn't keep the smoke contained," Martinez explained. "Because of the smoke and light, they must be placed at night, especially if we place them on the recoil mechanism or barrels of the cannons."

"What happens if we place a thermite grenade in the barrel of a cannon?" Adnet asked. "And what is the recoil mechanism on the cannon?"

"If the barrel of the cannon is exposed to such high temperatures, it will either bend or cause the barrel to partially collapse. If the cannon is fired, it will either send the shell in an incorrect direction or explode. It would be the same on the recoil mechanism. The thermite would basically weld the mechanism together, and if the weapon is fired, there would be no recoil. The cannon would be pushed backward by the shell into the operators behind the cannon," Martinez explained.

"Two-men teams should be used. While one team member places the grenades, the other team member can provide support or a diversion, if needed," Adnet added. "Especially if one team member is clumsy."

"Who are you calling clumsy?" Martinez asked. "I had the situation well under control until you threw that rock at the guardhouse. You couldn't even hit the guard at 10 yards."

"Get out of here," Blake interrupted the two men while trying to complete his report of the incident to Alsos Headquarters. "Go bother some Germans and try not to get caught."

Blake reported the successful operation but intentionally failed to mention the near capture of Adnet and Martinez. It was just another mission intended to disrupt enemy operations, not intended to end the war but to demoralize and make the Axis forces less effective. To that end, it was a successful mission.

Recent missions appeared to be more effective with the help of the Italian resistance. The OSS and MI6 were able to provide good information, but the local resistance provided better information and improved results.

"Do you think we should report recent German infiltration of local government offices?" Nate asked.

"Sure. The infiltration will make an Italian surrender more difficult," Blake reasoned. "A Nazi retreat or the surrender by the Italian government would unleash German squads to destroy the

Italian infrastructure, including roads, bridges, and probably local Italian leaders."

"You are probably right," Nate said. "The Nazi forces would execute local officials or citizens trying to stop the destruction."

"It is a real paradox where previous good friends or allies become enemies with the stroke of a pen on a surrender document," Blake added. "It becomes evident that the original intent of the joint efforts was basically to gain more real estate with no intent to benefit the citizens."

"Let's go get a beer," Nate injected.

Chapter 45

Axis Forces Moving

One of Enzo's cousins, Zita, was working with the German High Command group in Messina. Her job was pleasant enough, serving meals to the officers and helping host parties held frequently for visiting German and Italian officers. Recently, however, Zita noticed German treatment of Italian citizens and Italian soldiers was deteriorating to the point of outright disgust. Zita knew that Enzo was working with the local resistance and contacted him through a mutual friend at a local cantina.

Enzo was busy, but Roberto met with Zita the following day.

It was not good news to Roberto. German mistreatment of local citizens and Italian soldiers was increasing. It was common for German soldiers and officers to ridicule and even beat local citizens. They were in a retreat mentality and had been ordered to destroy many vital Italian assets left behind. Zita's information was not new, but her position serving the German command group was very interesting and could be used effectively.

Zita was asked to report any information concerning troop movements, visiting German dignitaries, or anything she felt would be of value to the resistance. She was more than willing to help.

Several days later, Zita contacted Roberto with information.

"While waiting tables for several German officers, I was

approached by a German sergeant," Zita explained. "He handed me a set of car keys and a description of a black Mercedes to bring to the front door for a German officer," Zita explained further. "I found the car as described but had to adjust the seat closer to the steering wheel to reach the pedals. While adjusting the seat, I found a briefcase under the seat. I quickly opened the case and read two documents before returning the briefcase to its original place."

Zita continued. "I drove the car around to the front door, parked, moved the seat back to its original position, and left the car running at the base of the steps leading to the restaurant. I found the sergeant, gave him the keys, and returned to my serving duties."

"Did you have any trouble with the sergeant?" Roberto asked.

"He accused me of spending too much time finding the car," Zita added. "I asked him if he knew how many black Mercedes were in the parking lot. He just smiled and took the keys."

"Did you have any other trouble?" Roberto asked.

"No, the last I saw of the sergeant, he was leading a German officer to the front door."

"Great work," Roberto said. "Can you describe the two documents you saw?"

"The first was a document outlining details of retreat to Mainland Italy at Messina. The document was addressed to a Gestapo colonel and outlined the process for placing mines on the two main roads leading to Messina, execution of several local officials, and destroying much of the port facility following the retreat of German and Italian troops."

Zita added, "The second was a description of an operation moving several divisions of troops to a new defensive line south of Rome. The line stretched from Minturno on the west coast to Vasto on the east coast. It was called the Gustav Line."

Zita explained, "That's all I remember of the papers. I hope the information will help." She thanked Roberto and returned to her duties at German High Command.

Chapter 46

AXIS FORCES INVADING SPAIN?

"Drop everything!" Colonel Powers ordered Sergeant Thomas at Headquarters in London. "Tell both Alsos teams to proceed to Gibraltar," Colonel Powers continued. "The Axis forces are moving several divisions of troops to the Spanish border. We need to know what they plan, how many divisions, makeup, entry point into Spain, and timetable for their advance on Gibraltar. The Allies are preparing for Operation Torch, and the Axis troops are moving toward Gibraltar. Could stop Operation Torch before it begins."

Sergeant Thomas made the arrangements for the two teams and returned to Colonel Powers' office. "I have ordered the teams to Gibraltar but will not have confirmation until midnight tonight," Sergeant Thomas continued. "Their moving toward Gibraltar will be slow and dangerous, but we should have an ETA tonight. I wonder why Axis forces are invading Spain. I thought Spain was neutral in this war."

"You are correct," Colonel Powers said. "Franco doesn't want to get involved. His country is still weak from the First World War, and he has factions in his own country that are rebelling and want to leave Spain and join France. Franco and Spain are unimportant to the Axis plans of occupying all of Europe."

"Franco doesn't want to side with the Allies for fear that they will invade Europe through his country," Sergeant Thomas suggested.

"What arrangements have you made for the teams while they are in Gibraltar?" Colonel Powers asked.

"I'm told by the OSS and British Intelligence that the British have carved out tunnels and caves in the Rock as a defensive measure and should provide a safe place for the teams to use while in Gibraltar," Sergeant Thomas answered. "How did we learn that the Axis forces are gathering at the Spanish border?"

"The Red Orchestra group out of Prague provided the information to the OSS," Colonel Powers answered. "Before you ask, the Red Orchestra is a group of anti-Nazi students and Communist Party members working to depose of the Axis regime."

"Is that the same group that has been printing and distributing anti-Nazi propaganda throughout Europe?" Sergeant Thomas asked.

"Yes, it is. They have published two pieces that I have read that were fascinating. The first was a Communist meeting report entitled "The Proper Care of Cactus Plants," and the second was the famous brown book of Hitler's terror and the burning of the Reichstag entitled *Electric Home Heating*."

"Didn't that group recently go underground when it became too dangerous to own a typewriter or hectograph?"

"I am told that you are right. In fact, by the time the group went underground, there are only thirteen of the original 421 members still active. Most were in prison or murdered."

"Sir, I'm not sure how effective the teams will be in reporting the Axis troop movements. If they are in Gibraltar, the teams will be 500 miles from the Spanish border."

"Good point, Thomas," Colonel Powers responded. "What do you suggest we do with the teams?"

"Team 1, aboard the submarine, is already close to the Strait of Gibraltar and out of position, while team 2 is moving to the southern coast of Sicily. Not much we can do with team 1, but team 2 is another matter."

"Why not have team 2 go ashore at Roses, Spain, just inside the Spanish border? They would be in a better position to monitor Axis troop movements."

"The Axis forces will have a hard time moving over the Pyrenees Mountains along the Spanish border unless they plan to cross the border at Eretria on the Atlantic coast or Roses on the Mediterranean coast."

"My guess is that the Axis forces will not attempt to cross the border over the mountains, which leaves the two coastal crossings the logical border crossing sites."

"Team 2 will be in position to monitor troop movements on the Mediterranean coast, while we could arrange for the OSS to monitor movements on the Atlantic coast," Colonel Powers added in agreement. "Great idea, Sergeant." As he left his office, Powers said, "I'm out of here. I'll be at OSS headquarters, if you need me. In the meantime, you make the necessary changes for both the Alsos teams and get an update on the status on Operation Torch and an ETA for the approach of the 1,400 ships approaching Gibraltar."

"Yes, sir, right away," Sergeant Thomas responded as he scrambled to his feet. "Just another mission to confuse or deceive the enemy. I hope we survive this to tell our grandkids," Sergeant Thomas whispered under his breath as the colonel left the office.

Chapter 47

GIBRALTA

"Gibraltar is not our focus now," Dino announced after receiving the encrypted message from Headquarters. "We are to proceed at full speed to the coastal town of Roses, just south of the Spanish border with France."

"What is Colonel Powers thinking?" John asked. "That must be 500 miles from Gibraltar. Even if we did find Axis troops in the area, we couldn't tell where they are heading."

"The message was clear. We are to go ashore at Roses to monitor any troop movements into Spain. Team 1 is now out of position to monitor German submarine movements while aboard a British submarine in the strait and heading south along the Moroccan coastline," Dino answered. "We will cover the southern route into Spain, while an OSS agent will monitor the northern route."

"I am so tired of this rocking back and forth and the constant smell of dead fish. I know it is necessary to maintain our cover as a fishing boat, but I am so ready for a hot shower and a steak," John responded.

"Maybe you should go complain to Nora. She might sympathize with you, especially since she has been doing this for almost three years now without much of a break. She lost a sister and most of her family at the hands of the Axis troops, and I'm sure she would console you over the really inconvenient fish smell."

"Okay. Okay." Dino finally stopped griping. "You are right, I am complaining needlessly, but your suggestion of going to see Nora is a good one. Maybe a glass of wine with a beautiful woman will improve my attitude."

As Dino approached the small control room, he could sense a difference in the air. The smell of dead fish had disappeared as he neared the bough of the boat. The smell of the seawater, the night's darkness, and now the increased wind helped make the night almost pleasant. "Where is Nora?"

Enzo was at the wheel, turned, smiled, and pointed in the direction of the bough where Nora was gazing into the night, watching for any indication of a patrol boat. Her hair was tucked under a small dark hat, but a few wild tufts flew free behind her inclined head as if staring at the stars.

"Good evening!" Dino shouted over the sound of the wind and waves.

No response. Once again, Dino shouted over the sound. Again, no response.

Dino then placed a hand on her shoulder. She jumped at first in response to an unfamiliar touch. She turned her head enough to see whose hand had invaded her solace then pressed her cold cheek against Dino's hand. Dino opened his heavy jacket and wrapped his arm and half of this jacket around her shoulders.

"Sorry, I didn't mean to startle you," Dino said into her ear.

"I'm glad you did. I'm cold and was about to ask Roberto to relieve me for a cup of something hot."

As the two made their way down to the galley, Nora asked Roberto to take her place at the bough. He shook his head and marched off toward the lookout location on the bough. There were new smells coming from the galley. It was John, busy cooking something that smelled Asian and wonderful.

"When did you learn to cook?" Nora asked as she and Dino sat at the small table in the galley.

"Japanese mother," John responded.

"It smells great, but I'm not sure I want to know what's in my dish," Dino said before tasting the contents of two small bowls.

"I didn't realize you were Japanese," Nora said.

"Half Japanese and half Italian," John responded. "My father left us when I was seven. My sister and I were born in San Francisco. We lived with my mother in a small flower shop where I learned to cook, sew, and keep house, while my mother kept the family in food and clothing by selling flowers.

"My mother is Japanese but, like me and my sister, born in the United States. It didn't matter to the authorities when Pearl Harbor was bombed, and we were placed in a wartime encampment or more like a prison with thousands of other Japanese. Most were born in the United States, but still, they were thought to be sympathizers of Japan."

"Dino actually saved my family from several more years in the encampment as he helped me become involved with the Manhattan Project and the Alsos missions as a journalist."

Chapter 48

HEADQUARTERS, LONDON

"Welcome, everyone," Colonel Powers said to begin the debriefing. "Let's begin by thanking our friendly hosts, the British Military and the OSS. They have kept us out of harm's way, provided transportation, provided different identities, and saved the lives of several of us over the past two years. They helped design and build many of the devices we used to either slow the advance of the enemy or destroy many of their assets."

Powers continued. "I thought you would like to review the many accomplishments your efforts and dedication provided to aid the Allies in removing the Axis forces from North Africa, Sicily, and Greece. I would be remiss not to mention the dedicated help of both the Italian and French resistance. We could not have completed many of the missions without your help.

"In no particular order of significance, I would like to mention some of the missions and accomplishments and several others that didn't work but led the way to incorporate changes in battle procedure . . .

"First: The British discovery of the tank *Sand Trap*. Corporal Aaronson was not able to join us, but his discovery during a vacation in Egypt saved many British lives by delaying a column of German tanks during the battle along the border with Egypt. You will be pleased to hear that Aaronson has been promoted again and received a commendation for his effort. Maybe they will learn to spell 'detour,' Colonel Powers continued. "It is ironic in many ways to think a single corporal with an idea helped save lives and defeat an enemy without firing a shot."

"Second: I know you all will remember the efforts of John and Dino in designing the camel turd mine cover. There are those who still dispute the effectiveness of such a diversion, mainly because of the order, but several commanding officers will swear that they effectively saved lives and stopped several enemy columns of tanks and supply vehicles. Unfortunately, John and Dino won't receive a commendation because they are not military personnel, but they sure are appreciated by this officer and probably the rest of you.

"Third: The sticky bomb and coal bomb, not new to warfare, but it took Nate to reintroduce them into the current inventory of weapons. Both devices were incorporated effectively with the French and Italian resistance. Many German and Italian tanks were either destroyed or damaged with no loss of life.

"Fourth: Both teams learned of and worked around the Germans use of triangulation to locate and destroy radios and radio operators. Their efforts helped develop the jamming device in use throughout Italy and Europe. I'm still hearing complaints of the food provided in both the depression and the lava field. Too much sand and not enough beer.

"Fifth: The British Jock columns were used effectively for the first time against advancing German troops and motorcycle sidecars armed with machine guns. Eventually, the Jock columns were renamed the Desert Rats.

"Sixth: Operation Torch, the preamble to the invasion of Normandy, was the first operation involving American troops in North Africa and the entry of the war in Europe. Both teams were helpful in communicating information about forces on land and in the water to enable Operation Torch to be a success.

"Seventh: The early identification of the only general that disappeared in Sicily. No trace of the general has been found.

"There are others that I won't mention that had an impact on the performance of the German military and others that were not reported. Sometimes it is best to just forget or ignore orders to discuss missions and their significance.

"In closing, I want to thank each of you and wish you the best of luck. I suppose you can say your vacations are over, and you can go home and let someone else finish the battle to rid the world of the Axis and the Third Reich.

"You can go home proud of your service."

"I am proud of each and every one of you, and I would deem it a pleasure to serve with you anywhere, anytime, again."

Acknowlegements

Breuer, William B. *Bizarre Tales from World War II.*

Breuer, William B. *Deceptions of World War II.*

Delaney, John P. *The Blue Devils in Italy.*

Goudsmit, Samuel. *Alsos.*

Mullaner, Elizabeth. *War Stories: Remembering World War II.*

Nelson, Anne. *Red Orchestra.*

Overy, Richard. *Why the Allies Won.*

Urban, Mark. *The Tank War.*

Wheal, Elizabeth Anne; Pope, Stephen; and Taylor, James. *Encyclopedia of the Second World War.*

Wikipedia.com

www.ingramcontent.com/pod-product-compliance
Lightning Source LLC
Chambersburg PA
CBHW051005140626
46546CB00016B/735